A HISTORY OF THE

BOSTON *Braves*

A TIME GONE BY

WILLIAM J. CRAIG

THE
History
PRESS

Published by The History Press
Charleston, SC 29403
www.historypress.net

Copyright © 2012 by William J. Craig
All rights reserved

First published 2012

Manufactured in the United States

ISBN 978.1.60949.857.3

Library of Congress CIP data applied for.

This book is dedicated to my father, John Edward Craig, a lifelong Braves fan, and his all-time favorite player, Alvin Dark. My father ensured that I would also be a Braves fan and never forget that they came from Boston. For this I am eternally grateful.

CONTENTS

PREFACE

As I wrote this book, I wanted to bring to life an era that too quickly passed us by. This was the era when the idea of the game mattered even more than the idea of winning. To those lucky enough to have passed through the Braves Field turnstiles, the Braves and Braves Field will always have a hallowed niche in the corridors of their collective memory. I hope this book will help to resurrect old memories, like the faces of old friends. Braves Field was where many a child learned about the fond expectancy of springtime and the harsh reality of autumn. This was the place where fans would relax in their seats and indulge in an old dream, like their fathers before them, while watching in relative solitude their often-inept heroes cavorting on the field. Here is where spectators and players were allowed to share a common experience. There was always the feeling that you were at home; you knew the players and other spectators—you were a community. Even though a community doesn't always think alike, it always shares a common ground.

The Braves ball club, although constantly overflowing with defeat, couldn't help but entrance us and make us care. Across the expanse of American history, baseball, with its memories and myths, gives us standards by which we constantly measure ourselves. The underlying factor for the writing of this book is historic preservation.

Baseball is an American odyssey that links an older generation to a younger generation. It helps us pass the best of ourselves down to the next generation. Baseball fans today are caught up in a nonstop multimedia three-ring circus. After writing this book, I found myself asking, has our great American pastime, along with the Boston Braves, faded into oblivion? The answer is heard in echoes from the past. These echoes tell us that what finally does endure is a lesson that every Boston Braves fan learned at an early age—some things are more important than winning!

ACKNOWLEDGEMENTS

I would like to take this time to thank the many people who have been instrumental in getting this book completed and published: Jeff Saraceno of The History Press, the Boston Braves Historical Association for the player/fan reunions and keeping the memory of the Boston Braves alive and well, the librarians at the Boston Public Library and the staff of the photo archives for all their help, the staff of the Revere Public Library, the staff at the Baseball Hall of Fame Archives and Boston University Archives. I would also like to thank my wife, Charlene, for typing this manuscript and my beautiful daughter, Meadow Jean, for understanding that Daddy had to work rather than play with her.

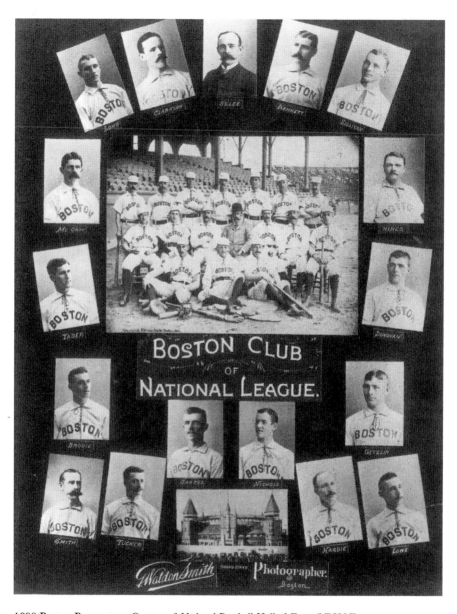

1890 Boston Beaneaters. *Courtesy of National Baseball Hall of Fame (NBHOF).*

INTRODUCTION

When I was born in 1972, the Boston Braves and Braves Field had been gone for almost twenty years—all that remained was the right field pavilion and the main entrance on Gaffney Street. My father grew up a Braves fan because of his father. When I was approximately five or six years old, he would put me to bed at night with stories of the Braves' glory days during the late thirties and into the early fifties.

I grew up believing that Tommy Holmes, Warren Spahn and Johnny Sain were the holy trinity of the baseball world and that Alvin Dark was the greatest shortstop who ever played the game. When we would drive by the old park, which is now Nickerson Field, I would try to picture the entire stadium still there and maybe even a game being played. From the earliest years of my life, I believed that Tommy Holmes could do no wrong, and I still do.

Braves Field has always been a mystical place to me; a shrine filled with past baseball gods and thoughts of what might have been. If you are a Braves fan, then I am sure you feel the same way I do. So sit back and follow me through this magical time warp, back to the Wig-Wam, back to when players arrived at the ballpark by trolley, back to when a seat in the bleachers only cost you sixty cents and the programs were a dime. Back to when the game was just a game and your children could look up to ballplayers as role models, long before greed and corporate corruption tainted our great American pastime.

CHAPTER 1

A MAN AND HIS PASSION

Happy is the man who can make his living out of his passion, assuming both to be legitimate. Happier still is he whose view of life is rich enough to go beyond a single pursuit to an embracing interest in human values in their broadest as well as most intimate aspects. This description fits Harry Wright. British-born Wright was the son of Sam Wright, a prominent professional cricketer in his day. Harry learned the game of cricket in Hoboken, New Jersey, at the Allesian fields. It is here that he began a love affair with the game of baseball. An unknown sportswriter once wrote, "Harry Wright breathes baseball and incorporates baseball in his players." In the mid-1800s, Wright moved to Cincinnati, Ohio, and was offered a job by Aaron B. Champion, owner of the Union Cricket Club. Wright accepted the job of bowler.

In 1865, Champion's interest was swayed toward baseball. He was the son of a prosperous merchant, and his talents included mercantile promotion, which he harnessed to his sports interest. In 1866, Wright switched from cricket to baseball and became the manager of Mr. Champion's Red Stockings.

The Cincinnati Red Stockings certainly weren't the first professional team, but they were the first to admit to paying their players. From the very beginning, Wright saw the game's commercial potential. The commercialism of baseball started out with the best of intentions and wound up a cesspool filled with greed and iniquities. When Harry Wright started out to commercialize the game, he wrote, "We must make the game worth witnessing, and there would be no fault found with the price…a good game is worth 50 cents, a poor one is dear at 25." He drilled his players in fundamentals and insisted they be silent and businesslike on the field. He is also credited for dressing them in knickers to increase their running speed. Once Wright felt that his players were ready for the public, he scheduled games across the country and took the team on a national tour. From 1867 to 1869 they went undefeated. In 1869, the Red Stockings finished the season with sixty-nine wins and not a single loss; and the profit that year...$1.39.

Harry Wright was a great player, besides being a successful American entrepreneur who could dream as audaciously as he pleased. Not only was he the chief architect of commercialized baseball, but he also hit 7 home runs in a single game. As amazing a feat as this may seem, Harry's brother George was even more astonishing as an athlete. George also has the distinction of being the first highest-paid player in baseball. He was paid $1,400 a season—$200 more than his brother Harry. In 1869, he hit .519, scored 339 runs and hit 59 home runs. An unknown sportswriter later recalled, "Whenever George would pull off one of those grand, unexpected plays that were so dazzling, his prominent teeth would gleam and glisten in an array of white molars that would put our own Teddy Roosevelt and his famed dentistry in the shadow."

The Red Stockings' star pitcher was Asa Brainard. He had good control but limited powers of concentration. Once, when a rabbit jumped out of the outfield grass, he ignored two men on base. Instead he wanted to see if he could hit the rabbit on the run. He missed the rabbit, and the two runs scored.

The Red Stockings' home park was the Lincoln Park Grounds, formerly known as the Union Cricket Club Grounds. The park was officially opened on May 4, 1869, and was used by the Red Stockings before the Major Leagues began in 1871.

Only one of Wright's Red Stockings actually came from Cincinnati; most were from New York. Almost all of his players were blue-collar guys. There were two hatters, two insurance salesmen, a bookkeeper and a piano maker.

The Red Stockings remained undefeated during the 1870 season. The Red Stockings were barely winning; even the collegiate baseball team of Harvard came close to defeating Cincinnati but failed.

On June 27, 1870, in Washington, D.C., just five years after the Civil War ended, Cincinnati catcher Doug Allison persuaded a saddle maker to fashion a padded buckskin glove for him before an exhibition game against the local Olympic Club. Allison used it that day, as his team beat the Olympic Club 35 to 24. Allison inadvertently changed the game of baseball forever, however slowly, to the point where a team in 1876 averaged six errors per game, while by 1988 teams were averaging fewer than one error per tilt.

Allison did not develop the glove to create a fashion statement. He created it to give his injured hand some protection from wicked fouls and the hard throws from his pitcher, Asa Brainard.

During the 1870 season, Wright scheduled a game between his team and the Brooklyn Atlantics. The Atlantics had once been a great team, but the Red Stockings were favored five to one. After all, they'd now played ninety-two games without a loss. Some fifteen thousand New Yorkers crossed the East River to Brooklyn by ferry and then took horse-drawn cars to the ballpark. "Hundreds who could or would not produce the necessary fifty cents for admission, looked on through cracks in the fence," reported *Harper's Weekly*. The game they saw seemed at first to be going the way the odds makers had predicted. Cincinnati got out to an early three-run lead, but Brooklyn came back with two runs in the fourth and two more in the sixth to snatch it back. At the end of nine innings the score was tied at five. The jubilant Atlantics started off the field, satisfied that they had held baseball's toughest team to a draw. Wright wasn't through; the rules, he said, clearly stated, "unless it be mutually agreed upon by the captains of the two nines to consider the game as drawn," a tie game must continue into extra innings. The Atlantics insisted they were more than satisfied with a draw. Wright appealed to the highest authority on hand, Henry Chadwick, chairman of the rules committee of the National Association, who ruled in his favor. Wright's gamble seemed to pay off; Cincinnati scored two runs in the top of the eleventh. Then the tension evidently became too much even for the Red Stockings. Asa Brainard gave up a single and later allowed the runner to reach third on a wild pitch. He then watched helplessly as the Atlantics first baseman, Joe Start, hit one into the crowd standing along the left field line. Left fielder Cal McVey managed to get his hand on it, but a run scored. The next batter drove in Start to tie the game up again. There was still a man on first and only one out. The next Atlantic batter hit a grounder to the Red Stockings' first baseman, Charlie Gould, who let the ball pass between his legs. Gould stumbled after it and then threw it over the third baseman's head as the runner raced home with the winning run.

After the game, Wright went to a Western Union office and sent this telegram to Cincinnati: "Atlantics, 8; Cincinnati, 7. The finest game ever played. Our boys did nobly, but fortune was against us. Eleven innings played. Though beaten...not disgraced."

The Cincinnati fans were devastated by the loss. The extraordinary streak was over. The fans stopped going to the games. The investors and the stockholders withdrew their holdings, complaining that, with attendance

The only team to play at the Congress Street Grounds from May 16, 1894, to June 20, 1894. They played here due to a fire at the South End Grounds. *Courtesy of Boston Public Library (BPL).*

down, the players' salary demands were unreasonable. Even the *Cincinnati Gazette* was disheartened with baseball, as it printed this statement: "Baseball mania has run its course; it has no future as a professional endeavor." Without the backing of the investors, the team could no longer sustain itself, and the end result was the disbandment of the team at the end of the 1870 season.

Wright, still believing in the value of professional baseball, took his dream and the remnants of the club to Boston. Wright moved the team at the invitation of a band of New England promoters. In Boston, Wright was guaranteed financial backing and fan patronage. So, in 1871, Wright enrolled his team in the National Association of Professional Base Ball Players, otherwise known as the "professional nine."

When Wright moved the team to Boston, he was quoted as saying, "Baseball is business now, and I am trying to arrange our games to make them successful and make them pay, irrespective of my feelings, and to the best of my ability." The Red Stockings made their debut in Boston on May 16, 1871, at the South End Grounds, which was formerly known as the Walpole Street Grounds, Union Baseball Grounds and the Boston Baseball Grounds.

CHAPTER 2

PROFESSIONAL BASEBALL COMES TO BOSTON

Boston was filled with anticipation concerning the 1871 season. Harry Wright's maiden Red Stockings started out by pounding Lowell 40–1, as Harry himself rapped out seven hits. The Red Stockings had expected to be a top contender for the pennant, but the team soon became dogged by injuries and unable to poke its collective nose much above the .500 mark. The most serious loss was shortstop George Wright, who suffered a leg injury in New York when he collided with left fielder Fred Cone while chasing a pop fly. The injury was not believed to be serious initially, but it was the same leg George had injured in 1870 and was slow to heal, causing him to miss sixteen games (half of his team's total). The injury would hamper him for the rest of his career.

With Wright benched because of his injury, second baseman Ross Barnes moved to shortstop, while Sam Jackson, a native of New England and a veteran of the New York amateur scene, moved in at second base. Jackson finished the season with a sub-.200 average, a precipitous decline from George's .409 mark.

Later in the campaign, other regulars fell victim to varying degrees of disability. Cal McVey was injured in a midseason game at Rockford. Fred Cone and Dave Birdsall limped around with minor nicks. Following a July loss to Troy, Wright decided to cancel some games and take time off to heal the wounded. Boston did not play another league game until August 3, nearly three weeks later. This type of behavior was common among the National Association entries since no formal schedule was drawn up prior to the season. An injury to a key player was sufficient cause to refrain from fulfilling previously scheduled engagements or to refuse to make new engagements.

As far back as 1871, Boston was plagued by player injury and financial stress. Even though Boston was one of the more successful organizations, it still felt the crippling effect of player leverage on salaries. Boston's player payroll, which totaled $14,500.00 in 1871, jumped by over $6,000.00 within five years. Harry Wright himself pulled down $2,500.00 as field captain and club secretary. Salary costs were only one of the labor expenses of fielding a competitive nine. On road trips, clubs absorbed charges of $1.00 a day per player for room and board and the same cost even at home for single players during the season. The Boston ledger included the costs of rooms at "Mrs. Parker's." One road trip cost the Red Stockings $1,161.03, although they did take in $3,537.22. These were just the beginning of Boston's financial problems, which would haunt the club until the move to Milwaukee in 1952.

The fierce rivalry that developed between Boston and the Athletics during the 1871 season only strengthened Wright's desire to capture the 1872 pennant. Because he had protested the Athletics' right to the pennant, manager Hayhurst of the Athletics had written Wright a sarcastic letter asking where his team ought to hang the streamer. Wright's reply was caustic: "If I had them," he said, "I should fly them both in all the games we play next season." He continued, "The proper place is or would be the Athletics' club room or someplace where all who wish could go and see them," instead of the saloon in which it presently hung. He advised Hayhurst to remember his obligation to "elevate the National Game" and, as the "first legal and recognized Champions of the United States," to remember that commercial baseball had a long way to go before it became financially profitable.

A few months later, Wright settled his Athletics account in grand style, with the two rivals in hot competition in midseason. All of Boston took half a holiday when the hated Athletics came to town. Betting odds were even, but Boston belied this by crushing its rivals 13–4. Among the game's highlights was a great catch by Harry Wright, who responded to cheer upon cheer by very politely lifting his hat! After that, nothing could stop the Red Stockings. They went on to post a final log of 39 and 8. This far outdistanced most rivals, and five discouraged entries dropped out before the season ended. In all, the six second-division clubs recorded only 16 victories out of 94 decisions. While these defections played havoc with attendance, Wright won a resounding vote of confidence from the Boston directors. It was also

Braves players Rabbit Warstler, Eddie Miller, Al Lopez, Les Scarsella and Chet Ross on the dugout railing at Braves Field. *Courtesy of BPL.*

around this time that Cincinnati had finally come to the realization that there would be no team in 1872 and no team in the immediate future. A large crowd gathered at the Union Grounds in Cincinnati for an auction of most of the Red Stockings' memorabilia. Aaron Champion, president of the club during its glory years, was there, as was a former secretary. The highest price ($40) was paid for a pitcher and goblet won in an 1867 tournament. The championship streamer of the undefeated 1869 team was sold for $7. A number of game balls brought anywhere from $1 to $5. When everything had been sold, the crowd departed, not to see professional baseball again until 1876. Boston, successor to Philadelphia as league champions, also succeeded them in the poor house, accumulating unpaid debts of more than $5,000, including accrued salaries.

During the winter of 1872, there were serious doubts regarding the ability of the Red Stockings to place a team on the field to defend their title. The catastrophic fire, which swept through the city in October, did nothing to alleviate the financial distress of the team or its backers. Harry Wright was forced to use all of his considerable persuasiveness to convince the incumbent Boston players to return the following season. He assured them that the unpaid 1872 salaries would be made up and told them that he himself would not have stayed if he was not confident of this fact.

During the winter of Boston's discontent, the citizens of Cincinnati engaged in a bit of gratuitous grave dancing. They made it known that, if the Boston team was disbanded, they had all intentions of bringing back the Wright brothers as the nucleus of a revived Cincinnati nine.

On December 11, 1872, more than 150 supporters met in Brackett's Hall in Boston to effect the salvation of their beloved champions. It was decided that the Boston Association, which had operated the team in 1872, would be effectively dissolved. In its place would be the Boston Base Ball Club, which would assume the debts of the Boston Association and sell new stock to raise funds for the 1873 season. All parties agreed to make concessions. The Boston Association stockholders relinquished majority control with the issuance of the new stock. The players were asked to accept their accrued salary in installments during the 1873 season. In return for their patience, it was proposed that the players receive a share of the profits (if any) at the end of the season.

The team survived the crisis, as an early southern trip replenished the barren treasury and enabled the new stockholders to begin making good on salary arrears. Much to the chagrin of its National Association opponents, the 1873 team was even stronger than the 1872 edition. The only notable departures were Cal McVey, who elected to sign with Baltimore, and team captain Charley Gould, who retired. All other key players returned to the fold. In addition, Harry Wright was able to do some grave dancing of his own, scooping up James White and Jim O'Rourke from the defunct Cleveland and Middletown clubs. Nineteen-year-old pitcher/outfielder Jack Manning, who had batted a robust .517 for the Boston Juniors, moved up to the big team. He replaced Froley Rogers, who retired from the game. Al Pratt of Cleveland was also offered a contract, but declined, feeling that the company was too fast.

With renewed hope, Wright launched a second pennant drive the following year. Although George Wright's rheumatism accounted for a sluggish start, two brilliant rookies, Jim O'Rourke and Jim "Deacon" White, took up the slack while showing the promise that would make them two of the mightiest stars of the century. By August the team was whole again but still stood ten games behind the front-running Philadelphia "Whites"—a new entry from Quakertown. A month of desperate pressing closed the gap to two and a half games, and although the Phillies hung on through September, they collapsed

Bob Elliott and Sid Gordon posing with an unknown child in 1951 in front of the Braves dugout at Braves Field. *Courtesy of BPL.*

in October after dropping five games in a row. One of the losses came at the hands of Boston before a crowd of five thousand Philadelphians.

On September 1, while fishing from a boat in New York Harbor near Fort Hamilton, twenty-three-year-old left fielder Albert Thake of the Atlantics lost his balance and toppled into the water. Although he was within swimming distance of the shore, Thake was not a swimmer and sank directly to the bottom. On October 23, Bob Ferguson organized an exhibition game between the old Cincinnati Red Stockings and the Old Brooklyn Atlantics. The proceeds were earmarked for Thake's widowed mother, who had been deprived of her only means of support. Despite the cooperation of the players from these legendary teams, threatening weather kept attendance to a minimum. A disappointed Ferguson was only able to turn over $200 to Mrs. Thake.

The Red Stockings returned to action and thrust themselves into the thick of the pennant race with five consecutive victories, including key wins over Chicago (September 5) and Philadelphia (September 9). In a 31–10 victory over Cleveland on September 2, Boston unloaded on the tired "Five-Inning Wonder" Al Pratt for twenty-three turns in the last two innings.

Boston's pennant-winning record in 1873 was 43 and 16. The tight pennant race probably explains why the National Association set a record for endurance. It was around this time that Wright set the pace for the owners of today, as he bought up stars as fast as the weaker franchises could produce them. In a time when economic depression cut attendance and caused smaller franchises to collapse, players, not owners, were more or less in charge of the league. Good players took to revolving, moving from team to team in search of better pay and steady work. Fans complained of drunken rowdiness at games, and there were rumors of carousing ballplayers and of staging games to suit gamblers. But Wright's team was above reproach. An excerpt from the *New York Herald*, paying them tribute for their honesty, read, "Above all they invariably play to win. The latter cannot be said of all the professional nines. Indeed to such low ebb have the morals of so many professional players descended that no man can now witness a game between many of the clubs and be sure that both sides are striving to win. Gamblers buy up one or more players to lose a game and its lost."

The 1874 season was shrouded in controversy due to rumors of gamblers paying players to throw games. The league fell victim to disinterest, mismanagement and financial distress because of Boston's easy victory in the pennant race.

Henry Chadwick, chairman of the National Association's rules committee, hurled charges of dishonesty toward some of the teams, noting that the number of questionable games must be kept on the level so as to maintain the public's faith in baseball. Chadwick was also quoted as saying, "Harry Wright was the father of professional baseball."

New charges of dishonesty continued to circulate as the 1875 campaign approached. Nevertheless, the spirit of the contenders ran high. In addition to seven holdovers from 1874, six other clubs paid the token entry fee and girded for action.

As for Wright's 1875 team, it was at its pinnacle of power, and the manager saw no reason for tinkering with the lineup. With such power waiting to be unleashed, Harry was understandably impatient for spring to arrive.

The winter was a cold one that carried into March—it would have been better for the rivals if it had never ended. Except for Chicago and the Athletics, who fought well, the other ten teams were hopelessly outmatched. As the defeated ten watched gate receipts and dreams fade, some openly demanded the breakup of Wright's team. This type of unrest wasn't pleasant, but a greater threat to the league was the conflict stirred up by the Force case.

A celebrated revolver, Dave Force jumped a Chicago contract to play with the Athletics; and when Chicago's formal protest was disallowed, Wright entered the fight. He accused the Athletics of using the circuit's arbitration committee to its own advantage. Soon tensions caused by the dispute spilled over onto the playing fields. On several occasions, players and spectators engaged in bitter brawls. In Philadelphia, crowds surged onto the playing field and harassed Boston fielders. Spectator conduct was no better in Boston. It took diplomacy on the part of the battling directors to restore order to the league and the name of sportsmanship. Finally, by midseason, tempers cooled and clubs returned to playing baseball, an enterprise in which Boston's superiority was obvious.

In driving his club to its fourth straight pennant, Wright crushed all opposition. In no other Major League campaign did a team's superiority show as in that of the 1875 Red Stockings. Of the association's twenty leading hitters, eight were Boston men, including the top four. That season, Harry Wright was the only Boston regular to average fewer than one safe hit a game, as he was nearing the end of his active career. Also noteworthy is the fact that in an age of barehanded fielding, Boston fielding records approached modern standards.

Along with Spalding's pitching, such prowess carried Boston to a record of 71 and 8, and the team finished fifteen games ahead of its nearest rival. Clearly the association's lack of balance was killing commercial baseball as a spectacle. Promoters knew this, and before the 1875 season ended, some were conspiring to end both the rickety association and the Boston tyranny.

In 1875, Boston's player payroll was $20,685.60. Not until the 1880s would players' salaries or club payrolls surpass this mark. However, one must remember that players, rather than investors, were reaping the biggest rewards under the association. It is quite possible that high salaries frightened investment capital away from a players' league. Wright believed that this may be so and suggested that good talent could be had for much less. He thought high salaries spoiled players and held back the progress of big-time baseball. He was also quoted as saying, "What do the majority of the players do with all the money? Spend it foolishly to the injury of themselves, and consequently to the club engaging them, or with which they are playing."

In truth, investors did pocket fewer profits than players. After losing $3,000.00 in 1872, Boston showed a net profit of $4,020.38 in 1873. However, most of the latter gains were plowed back into the club, leaving a true profit of $767.93. In 1874, the club again netted a modest sum, this time $833.13. Finally, in 1875, when the club netted $3,261.07, the stockholders voted not to take dividends but rather to return the money to the club. Such behavior typified the era of gentleman professionalism and contrasts sharply with the mercenary philosophy of today.

The association era spearheaded the development of Major League Baseball as a latter-day entertainment business. In grappling on a small scale with such modern administration problems as advertising, plant operation, equipment, travel scheduling and salary negotiations, Boston had a total 1875 operating cost of $34,505.99. Though modest by today's standards, this total was larger than that of any previous association year, and it certainly showed the way for larger operations.

In many ways, this era was a proving ground for later business operations. As Boston's manager, Wright became an expert in administration by investigating the significance of road costs, uniforms and plant management. On the road he allowed just $1.00 a day for each man's room and board. By modern standards this is unthinkable, yet for $1,161.03, a dozen Red Stockings spent twenty days in hotels and had their food and travel too. On one trip, Boston grossed $3,537.22 from gate receipts, which shows the profits to be made in 1875.

When playing at home, Wright arranged room and board for his bachelor players for $1.00 a day at Mrs. Parker's. Wright also became a first-rate baseball quartermaster. In those years, the Red Stockings used cricket flannel, which cost up to $3.50 a yard. The shirts were made of American flannel and were contracted to George Wright's sporting goods outlet. Figuring that each man wore three uniforms a year, Wright shrewdly ordered all uniforms in three basic sizes so that a man could find parts to fit any uniform when necessary.

The Boston manager's wide knowledge and experience in baseball matters caused others to seek advice from him. Such requests were eagerly and willingly answered and covered a wide range of problems concerning baseball management. Wright gave advice on how to lay out a baseball diamond, including suggestions on seating construction, infield grading and the best kind of grass to plant in the outfield. He was a successful manager in an age when it took unusual ability to run a successful franchise under the rickety association. Nevertheless, he cast his lot with rebels seeking to build a better order. Wright entered this conspiracy because he believed the association to be a disciplinary failure. He found it incapable of exploiting the vast profit potential of this leisure outlet. "Professional teams," he wrote to arch conspirator Hulbert, "to keep in existence, must have gate money, to receive gate money they must play games, and to enable them to play games, their opponents must have faith that such games will prove remunerative."

Grateful for Wright's backing, Hulbert pronounced Wright's ideas for reform to be sound and that they would one day earn Wright the title of "father of the game." But this honor Wright brushed aside with drollery, saying that it made him feel old and, more seriously, that Chadwick had the better claim.

William Hulbert was the owner of the Chicago ball club and the driving force behind the creation of the National League. Wright, Chadwick and Hulbert all designed strict policies for the National League. These policies being that players were forbidden to drink (on or off the field), no beer was to be served at the parks, gambling was forbidden, ticket prices were set at fifty cents and no games were to be played on Sundays. The team owners wanted full control. They wanted to have an employer/employee relationship with the players. Hulbert and the other eight owners in the league also added a reserve clause to the contracts of the five best players of every team. This clause required that each player play only for his current employer and in effect "reserved" his services in perpetuity. Players who objected were fired and blacklisted. To some it may seem that the National League was very authoritarian, but remember this was during a time when baseball owners relied solely on fans for patronage and profit. They had to run the league this way in order to keep the public's faith in commercial baseball and guarantee the success of their investments. I can't help but wonder what these founding fathers of Major League Baseball would say if they saw how the leagues are run by today's owners.

When William Hulbert was questioned about the salary cap of $1,400, his reply was honest and straightforward: "It's ridiculous to pay a ballplayer $2000 a year, especially when the $800 boys often do just as well."

In looking over Wright's record from 1866 to 1875, one is left with the impression that the achievement was a logical outcome of virtuous practices like clean living, hard practice and honest capitalism. However, even the briefest study of source materials leads one to conclude that the Red Stockings were quite human. Manager Wright's personal record shows that no one knew more than him about the mixed joys and sorrows of managing this club. Although Wright's men were well trained and disciplined, they also gave their manager many hard times. At times they straggled, missed trains and ducked out on practices. Pitcher Asa Brainard was a leading offender, but others, including Harry Wright's own brother George, cut practice sessions. Brainard's temperament led him into a maze of troublemaking channels and made him difficult to manage. In those days, physical exertion was more a part of work than now, and baseball pitchers were expected to work all of the games.

Yet it was Wright's misfortune to be saddled with a hypochondriac pitcher, who often complained of imaginary ailments. At times every member of this super team needed bracing; one general problem was keeping them away from the whiskey. Although Wright was a temperate man, he realized that total abstinence ran counter to the prevailing American belief that ability to hold liquor was a measure of manliness. All the troubles of years past would soon be forgotten, as the dawning of a new era was about to begin.

CHAPTER 3

MIRACLE BRAVES

The National League's first game was played on April 22, 1876. George Wright, the shortstop for Boston, was the first man to bat, and his teammate Jim O'Rourke recorded the first hit. Boston defeated Philadelphia 6–5.

It was more than an auspicious debut for the Boston team, which was to experience its golden age before the turn of the century. The first year in the National League the team won 39 games and lost 31. It finished fourth that first year and drew about sixty-five thousand in attendance. In 1876, Boston had a net loss of $777.22; this loss was not as bad as what some of the others reflected in the league.

In 1877, Nathaniel T. Apolonio sold the team to Arthur H. Soden. Soden's name became a synonym for Boston baseball, and his cash grants to clubs in financial distress helped the league to survive those first few years. Harry Wright became Soden's secretary and was obliged to haggle with hotel managers over something like an alleged $1.67 overcharge on Soden's bill.

Certainly Soden kept Wright under surveillance, for in negotiating the 1878 contract with catcher Pop Snyder, Wright told the catcher to name his terms, "but let them be moderate, and in accordance with the times."

Boston player James "Deacon" White, who posted a batting average of .358, won the National League batting championship of 1877. Harry White, the brother of Deacon, steered Boston toward pennants in 1877 and 1878.

The 1877 season's net losses doubled in comparison to the 1876 losses. In 1877, the club's net loss was $2,230.85, but elsewhere economy was the watchword as salaries were cut. Protesting players were blacklisted along with those suspected of crookedness. Adding to the atmosphere of fear was a challenge from a rival organization, the International League, which sought to establish itself as a major league.

Against this gloomy setting, Harry Wright drove his Red Stockings to the 1878 pennant. It was his last Major League championship, and it came in a year in which there was little glory or cash to accompany victory. Wright's Red Stockings finished the season with a 41 and 19 record.

The 1878 season was a landmark in Major League history in that it marked the first time each team in a commercial league completed its full schedule of games. However, managerial austerity, salary cuts and new stock issues created a discouraging picture. Ranked alongside the modestly profitable association era, it goes far to debunk the myth of league superiority.

From 1876 to 1880, at no time did Boston's home receipts match the association's record of $3,933.93 set in 1875. Furthermore, in the early years of the league, only once did Boston's payroll hit $18,814.00. In 1879, the austerity policy drove it down to $15,759.92. By the following year, it had dropped to $14,007.96. If the trend had continued, Boston salaries would have soon dropped below the seasonal total of the 1869 Cincinnati pioneers.

The economy's axe struck at several areas, including advertising (down from $1,440 in 1875 to only $873 in 1879), clubroom upkeep (cut from $1,626 in 1875 to $551 in 1880) and travel expenses (down from a princely $6,808 in 1875 to $2,813 in 1880). The drastic cut in travel accommodations was so damaging to player morale that, in one incident, Wright faced near mutiny. Because of this, the Soden administration decided to fire Wright.

The Boston Red Stockings started to become known as the National League Beaneaters. Their home field was the South End Grounds, Boston's first and only double-decked grandstand ballpark.

In 1883, there was another pennant race that would set the pattern for future Boston pennant winners. Three fifth-place finishes and sagging attendance prompted Soden to open his wallet and purchase Michael "King" Kelly for $10,000 from Chicago.

Kelly was considered by many to be Ty Cobb's superior on the bases. He also inspired the immortal cry, "Slide, Kelly, S-L-I-D-E." Kelly was the Ty Cobb and Babe Ruth of his time. In the late 1880s and early 1890s, he was known far and wide as the "Ten-Thousand-Dollar Beauty." That was his salary, but Kelly was a bargain. No ballplayer had the astounding ability or the color on and off the field that he had. A tall, powerfully built and handsome Irishman with a flowing mustache, Kelly was the idol of a nation. He was the

South End Grounds, 1892. *Courtesy of NBHOF.*

first ballplayer people followed on the streets. Boston fans were so delighted to get him that they gave him a house and a beautiful carriage drawn by ten glistening white horses so he could ride to and from the ballpark in style. Kelly's Boston contract was the richest in baseball and the first to officially recognize a player's profit-making potential off the field. In addition to $2,000 for playing, he got another $3,000 for "use of his picture." He earned still more money between seasons telling baseball stories from the vaudeville stage and reciting "Casey at the Bat" to audiences who saw him as the real-life embodiment of the poem's hero. Kelly often walked down the street twirling his cane as though he were the entire population, his ascot held by a giant jewel and his patent leather shoes painted as sharply as Italian dirks.

Kelly broke into baseball playing with a sandlot team for $3 a week, but before he was twenty he was playing with the Chicago White Stockings— and receiving a salary of $10,000! Kelly was a remarkable outfielder and a terrific slugger, with a batting average always hovering around .400. He was also the quickest-thinking ballplayer in all of history.

Special rules had to be made to curb the lightning-fast mind that would snatch winning ballgames from the opposition. Kelly sometimes skipped second on his way to third when the umpire was not looking. When he eventually shifted from the outfield to behind the plate, and opposing runners were about to slide into home, he liked to confuse them by covering the plate with his mask. He also liked to secretly signal the right fielder to move in before he made an apparently wild throw over the first baseman's head. The runner would then start for second, not realizing the ball would be caught and relayed for an easy out.

One afternoon, in the season of 1889, Charlie Ganzel was catching for Boston while Kelly (then captain of the team) was sitting on the bench. The rival batsman hit a high fly. It was a foul traveling down in the direction of third base. Ganzel set out to get the ball, but it was obvious that he could never reach it. Suddenly, quick as a flash, King leaped from the bench, rushed out on the field and announced in a loud voice, "Kelly now catching for Boston!" Then, with all the nonchalance in the world, he caught that high foul fly and retired the side to squelch a rally. After that bit of quick thinking on Kelly's part, the baseball fathers had to adopt a new rule that permitted no change of players in the course of a game, unless such changes were announced to the spectators by the umpire.

Kelly drank as hard as he played. When asked if he drank while playing he answered, "It depends on the length of the game." While King Kelly was an amazing ballplayer in many respects, it was the art of base running in which he was positively a genius. Baseball fans often came just to see him steal bases; for when Kelly ran, he never gave infielder or catcher anything more than the tip of his toe to tag. When stealing, he was the first to use the fadeaways, fall-aways, hook slides and other tricks that no other ballplayer could copy. He could circle the bases in about twelve seconds. He was one of the best-dressed men of his period and a lordly spender. No matter how much money he made, he was always broke. Eventually, his baseball bosses became so fed up with his royal temperament and wild escapades that he was suspended from the game. Kelly's wild living finally caught up with him in 1894, when he came down with a deadly bout of pneumonia. Most of his fair-weather friends deserted him. He was only thirty-seven when he died.

In 1888, Arthur Soden purchased John Clarkson (another Chicago player) for another $10,000, forming what was called the "$20,000 Battery."

Frank Selee became Boston's manager in 1890. His twelve-year reign would result in nine first-division finishes and five pennants. Greats such as King Kelly, base stealers Billy Hamilton and Harry Stovey and Bobby Lowe (the first player to hit four home runs in a game) spurred the Boston offense. The team also had Hugh Duffy, whose .438 average in 1894 is the highest in baseball history.

Boston owed much of its success in the 1890s to Charlie "Kid" Nichols's speedball, breaking ball and sharp-breaking curve. The Beaneaters finished first in 1891, 1892, 1893 and 1898. The "Kid" won thirty or more games a season during each of those years.

During these glory years, the ball club seemed to ooze with talented players such as Dan Brouthers, who, like Ruth, started out as a pitcher. In 1879, he was signed by the Troy Trojans, and after several unsuccessful pitching attempts, he became a full-time first baseman. Brouthers won five batting titles and led the league at one time or another in every major batting department. In the Majors, Brouthers initially struggled at the plate, so in 1880, he returned to semi-pro ball. Just one year later, he returned to the National League to stay.

In 1881, he signed with Buffalo, where he was teamed with Deacon White, Hardy Richardson and Jack Rowe. This quartet eventually came to the Hub to play for the Beaneaters. Boston is also where Brouthers captured his third batting title. His career batting average was .342. He was elected to the Hall of Fame in 1945.

In 1890, the club signed a rookie pitcher by the name of Charles "Kid" Augustus Nichols. Nichols, who received his nickname for his youthful appearance, would go on to become one of the greatest pitchers in history. Frank Selee, who was also his manager in Omaha, was the one who brought Nichols to the Beaneaters. In his rookie season, Nichols won twenty-seven games. He had ten straight winning seasons, which only added to Boston's success. When he came to the big leagues, Nichols only had one pitch—a fastball. Not until later in his career would he develop a seldom-used changeup pitch. It was Nichols's superb control that helped him become the youngest pitcher in Major League history to win three hundred games.

After 1898, the club began to decline due to owner Arthur Soden's refusal to match American League salary offers for his top players. As a result, several stars left, including Nichols, who quit the club and bought a part interest in the Kansas City team in the Western League.

The Beaneaters played at the South End Grounds until May 15, 1894, when a fire destroyed the park during the bottom of the third inning of the Beaneaters-Orioles game. The fire started in the right field bleachers. From May 16 to June 20, they occupied the Congress Street Grounds. The new park was smaller and only had a single-decked grandstand. The park at the South End Grounds had been severely underinsured, and there wasn't enough money from the insurance claim to build a park of equal size.

Many top players have plied their trade in Boston's National League franchise, but no player was more enterprising than pitching star Albert Goodwill Spalding, who would soon become the game's preeminent entrepreneur. Spalding borrowed $800 from his mother to open a sporting goods business. He began by manufacturing baseballs and paid the National League $1 for every dozen its teams used. This enabled him to advertise his product as the "official" league ball. Spalding liked to say in later years, "Everything is possible to him who dares."

In 1901, Pilgrims owner (the name Red Sox would come much later) Charles Somers lured some of the Beaneaters' top players over to his team and the newly founded American League. The National League had a salary cap of $2,400 for its top players in 1901, while the American League owners were offering salaries as high as $4,000 to $5,000 at a time when the average annual income was less than $700.

In March 1901, the Pilgrims walked away with several of the Beaneaters' top players, including outfielders Buck Freeman, Chick Stahl and Jimmy Collins, who some claim was the game's greatest third baseman. When Collins was questioned about his rationale for jumping from one Boston team to another, he replied, "I like to play baseball, but this is a business for me and I can't be governed by sentiment." The Pilgrims signed him to a $4,000 contract that year.

Beaneaters owner Arthur Soden was quoted in 1901 as saying, "Only one club will survive this battle in Boston, and that will be the same old National League." Soden was partially right. Only one club survived, but it wasn't the Beaneaters.

The beginning of a new century was a hopeful time for America, but the only thing Boston National Leaguers could look forward to was change bred of failure. There were five eighth-place finishes from 1903 to 1912. The Dovey brothers came in as new owners in 1906. The next season, the club had a new name, the "Doves." Four years later, William Hepburn Russell became owner and again the club's name was changed, this time to the "Rustlers." The name "Braves" was finally reached in 1912 when James Gaffney purchased the team. Gaffney was a member of the powerful political machine Tammany Hall, whose members were known as the Tammany Hall Braves.

Baseball is a game where anything can happen and any team can get hot for seven games. This is exactly what happened in 1914 to create the most remarkable upset in World Series history.

Overflow crowds spilling onto the field from the left field pavilion at Braves Field. *Courtesy of author's collection.*

It all started in July of that year, just before World War I began. The Braves started their march from the basement to first place. The team was backed by the pitching trio of Tyler, James and Rudolph, a trio as dear to Boston as Tinker, Evers and Chance to Chicago. The hot streak continued through the summer, with the Braves reaching fourth place on July 21 and second place on August 12. They finally passed the Giants on September 8, moving them into first place. The closing drive of 34 wins in 44 games led the Braves to the National League pennant and made gods out of a collection of misfits managed by George Stallings, a one-time medical student with a furious temper and gentle manner mixed together.

Stallings was also a master of baseball strategy. He platooned most positions as he had only three full-time regulars: first baseman Butch Schmidt, second baseman Johnny Evers and shortstop Rabbit Marranville. The spark plugs of the team were Evers and Marranville. Stallings also had three pitching aces to rely on: Dick Rudolph, Bill James and Lefty Tyler. Rudolph won twenty-seven games with control and a sharp curve. Tyler, a southpaw, had sixteen wins, while James used his speed to win twenty-six games.

The club worked hard to earn the title "The Miracle Braves," and they were the favorites of the press. The opposing Athletics had been to the series before and had the more proven players. This also made them the overwhelming favorites by choice to take the series. That didn't stop the Braves. They charged like a freight train into the series. The Athletics couldn't slow them down at all—never mind stopping them.

The first two games were scheduled for Philadelphia. The series opener was a duel between Rudolph and veteran Chief Bender. Rudolph scattered five hits to the Mackmen, but the Braves' hitters chipped away at Bender for two runs in the second inning and one in the fifth, finally knocking him out of the box with three in the sixth.

The biggest surprise of the 7–1 Boston win was the single, double and triple collected by catcher Hank Gowdy, a .243 hitter during the season. The Athletics now knew the Braves were for real, but that realization didn't help them any. Bill James blew the ball past the Athletics all afternoon in the second game, giving up only two hits. Philadelphia pitcher Eddie Plank was less untouchable and kept the plate undented until the top of the ninth. After Marranville struck out, Charlie Deal, a .210 hitter playing only because Red Smith broke his ankle in the last week of the season, hit a long fly to center that Amos Strunk misplayed into a double. After James fanned Les Mann, a .247 swinger dropped a Texas League fly past second baseman Eddie Collins to score the only run of the game.

After their two wins in Philadelphia, the Braves took over the role of favorite. The Braves' usual home park, the South End Grounds, was a shabby, run-down stadium, so the team borrowed Fenway Park from the Red Sox. The third game drew an attendance of 35,520 fans to see another mound duel between Lefty Tyler and Joe Bush. After nine innings, the score was knotted at 2–2. The Athletics got to Tyler for two runs in the top of the tenth, but the Braves sent the game on by answering with two runs. James relieved Tyler for the eleventh inning, and the Braves won it in the twelfth on a double by Gowdy and a throwing error by Bush, which allowed pinch runner Mann to score.

The Braves now had the force of a hurricane coming off the harbor— nothing could stop the four-game sweep, which concluded as Rudolph won the game in a 3–1 victory for the Braves.

Winning the World Series was the cap to an unbelievable .545 series batting mark for catcher Gowdy, who led all batters. As far as the Athletics

1914 Miracle Braves. *Courtesy of NBHOF.*

A Braves fan mocking Connie Mack's Athletics during the 1914 World Series at Fenway Park. *Courtesy of BPL.*

Pitcher Bill James. *Courtesy of NBHOF.*

1914 Miracle Braves in their warm-up jackets. *Courtesy of author's collection.*

were concerned, their team batting average of .172 speaks for itself. The Braves not only beat Connie Mack's highly favored American League Champions but humiliated them in four straight. This was a Braves team that was languishing in the gutter as late as July 19, while the Athletics, losers of only four games in the series of 1910, 1911, and 1913, had won another comparatively easy flag, defeating the second-place Boston Red Sox by eight and a half games.

The Braves were not a great team by any means, but their momentum led them on the most amazing climb in Major League history. Despite the Braves' big finish, the Athletics were inclined to be contemptuous of them. Connie Mack sent Chief Bender to scout the Braves in a late season game in New York. Mack learned later that Chief had gone fishing instead. When Mack reprimanded him, Bender replied with a broad smile, "We don't need to scout that bush-league outfit."

After the miracle of 1914, a season of darkness descended on the Braves. They dropped from second place to third place and then back into the basement.

CHAPTER 4
BRAVES FIELD

James Gaffney called it "the perfect ballpark" when he abandoned the old South End Grounds on Walpole Street and built Braves Field for $600,000 in 1915. The description was ridiculous to say the least. The fences were too far, and a succession of owners would alter the boundaries almost constantly (often to suit the team's power hitter of the moment). However, this usually backfired, as enemy hitters just swatted more cheap home runs. The concrete stands couldn't be moved and were too far from the action. The wind blew in from the Charles River, often carrying a film of soot and ash from the coal-burning trains in the railroad yard behind the outfield. Ty Cobb visited the new ballpark and emphatically stated, "No homerun will ever go over that fence." His prediction stood for two years for an over-the-fence home run and almost ten years for one to clear the left field fence.

The most famous section of the ballpark was a small section of bleachers in right field. It seated two thousand people and came to be known as "The Jury Box." This section was named by a sportswriter who noticed that it contained just twelve spectators during one game.

Perhaps the friendliest feature of the park was an arrangement with the transit authority that allowed the trolleys from Commonwealth Avenue to bring fans right into the ballpark.

When the Braves left the South End Grounds on August 11, 1914, they existed in limbo over at Fenway Park. They were guests of the Red Sox for over a year and remained so until Boston defeated St. Louis 3–1 before a packed house on August 18, 1915.

View of the left field pavilion from the grandstand at Braves Field. *Courtesy of author's collection.*

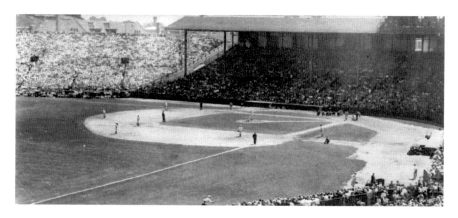

An afternoon game at Braves Field. Notice the roof on the grandstand—this photo was taken before rooftop seating was added in the late thirties. *Courtesy of author's collection.*

Braves Field

In 1915, Braves Field hosted its first World Series; but the Braves weren't involved—it was the Red Sox. When the Braves ball club had played in the series the year before, the Red Sox let them use Fenway Park for their home games, so the Braves reciprocated by letting the Red Sox use Braves Field as their World Series home park in 1915 and 1916. Hopes ran high in 1915 for an all-Boston World Series since both teams were in the thick of their respective pennant races, but it never happened—not that year, not ever.

The years 1917 to 1920 were Stallings's last four with the club. The team averaged a winning percentage of .429. Fred Mitchell became manager in 1921 and brought the Braves to fourth place that year. Plagued by player and owner uprooting, Boston would lead the second-place division of the National League only twice until after the Second World War.

On May 1, 1920, the Braves and Brooklyn (not the Dodgers, the Robbins—the name Dodgers would come much later) battled it out for twenty-six innings before it was called a 1–1 tie due to darkness. Brooklyn's Leon Cadore and Boston pitcher Joe Oeschger both pitched what could only be compared to a triple-header. This is still the longest game ever played in Major League history, and as if this weren't unbelievable enough, they only used three balls the entire game! Duels between Boston and Brooklyn were more than plentiful. The two teams played twenty-three innings in 1940. Another remarkable feat occurred in 1923 at Braves Field when Boston shortstop Ernie Padgett executed one of only eight unassisted triple plays in Major League history.

Roger Hornsby circa 1928.
Courtesy of NBHOF.

James Gaffney's park remained conducive to inside-the-park home runs. For example, in 1921, 34 out of 38 home runs were in the park. On April 29, 1922, the Giants hit four of them. Everywhere else in the country fans were going wild for the excitement of the out-of-the-park home runs Babe Ruth was swatting every chance he got. So, in 1928, the Braves management finally conceded to fan demand and changing times. They pulled the outfield fences in by installing new bleachers in center and left field. By doing this, they shrank the home run distance from 550 feet dead center to 387 feet and from 402 feet down the foul lines to 320 feet in left and 364 feet in right. Unfortunately, the new dimensions caused a rain shower of home runs to fall in the new left field bleachers. This is also around the time when third baseman Les Bell, a right-handed batter, came within inches of swatting four home runs in one game. He hit three into the left field bleachers and a triple that almost made it.

Long before Bill Veeck came up with the idea (or admitted to it after the fact) of moving the fences in and out at Cleveland late at night, the Braves had this idea.

The dimensions of the field changed annually, although some people claimed daily. As a result of Les Bell and countless other power hitters, the new bleachers in center field and left field were removed, and an eight-foot-high wooden fence was put up inside the original concrete wall. Over the years, the center and left field bleachers reappeared and disappeared again and again.

Eventually, home plate and the entire right field foul line shifted twenty-five feet to the right, causing part of the right field pavilion to be blasted out in order to secure a reasonable distance between the pavilion and the right field line.

During the 1920s and even into the 1930s, the Braves teams were considered underdogs. They were constantly in financial trouble and in trouble in the league standings. In seventy-six years of the club being in Boston, only two Braves ever won batting championships, each in their only season wearing a Braves uniform. The first of these two was Roger Hornsby, who batted .387 as a player/manager in 1928.

The second catcher was Ernie "Schnozz" Lombardi, who hit .330 in 1942. Both players requested that the club trade them after they won the title, and both players were accommodated.

In 1930, a rookie right-hander named Wally Berger came to the club. He hit thirty-eight home runs in his rookie season, which is still a Major League record and the most ever by a Boston Brave. Berger's fame among

Braves Field

Braves Field circa 1930. The view from the left field pavilion looking toward the "Jury Box." Notice the temporary stands in the outfield. *Courtesy of BPL.*

Rabbit Marranville on the start of his twenty-third Major League season. *Courtesy of BPL.*

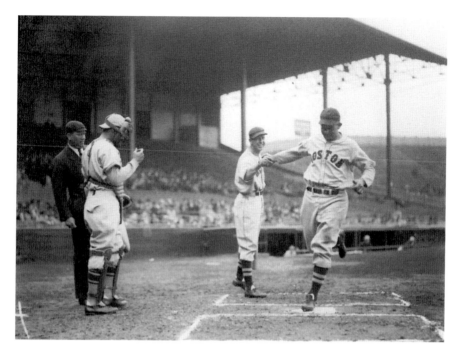

Unknown Red Sox player crossing home plate at Braves Field during a preseason City Series game. *Courtesy of BPL.*

the fans wasn't truly clinched until the final game of the 1933 season, when he hit what many call the most dramatic home run of his career—a pinch-hit grand slam that cinched the game and put the Braves in fourth place. Consequently, this was their only first-division finish between 1921 and 1946.

Berger also hit more home runs than anyone at Braves Field, with 105. He was also the starting center fielder for the National League in the 1933 and 1934 All-Star Games. During the 1933 season, the Braves lit a flame to an otherwise drab regular season. Manager Bill McKechnie had the Braves in second place behind the Giants by just six games. The Braves were scheduled to play the Giants in a double-header on Labor Day weekend. The Braves won the opener to bring it within five games. The next day, fifty thousand fans made their way to the park for the double-header. Gaffney Street was overflowing with fans. More than ten thousand customers had to be turned away. As usual, the Braves couldn't keep the flame lit and lost both games to the Giants.

Around this time, the Boston Braves started another gimmick in hopes of boosting attendance. This gimmick, which came to be known as "The

Knothole Gang," became a thirty-year fixture in the left field pavilion and gave countless kids a chance to see their first Major League game.

Everyone knows that George Herman "Babe" Ruth started his career in Boston with the Red Sox, but what few know is that Ruth ended his career in Boston with the Braves. Ruth signed with the Braves in 1935 after being released from the Yankees. Judge Emil Fuchs, who was the owner at the present time, needed a gimmick to help save his ailing franchise from falling attendance. Ruth was just what he needed. He bamboozled Ruth into signing by offering him empty titles such as vice-president, assistant manager and active player. There was also the phony promise that in 1936 he would take over the position of manager from Bill McKechnie. This was the job that Ruth had dreamed about for years. The Babe started the 1935 season in his usual flair on opening day. He singled and homered off Giants pitcher Carl Hubbell to drive in three runs in a 4–2 Boston victory.

Soon after, however, Ruth realized his health was hindering his performance. He could no longer run the bases, and it was obvious that Judge Emil Fuchs was just using him as a sideshow to raise attendance. So on June 2, 1935, Ruth called for a press conference in the clubhouse at Braves Field and announced his retirement as an active player. Fuchs made a feeble attempt to save the club's reputation, along with his own, by claiming that he fired Ruth that same day!

Fuchs added to the team's ruin in more ways than one. In 1929, he appointed himself manager and directed the team in street clothes from the bench, with the assistance of Johnny Ever. This move was mocked highly by both the fans and the press, especially since Fuchs did this so he could save on a manager's salary.

The 1930s were a bleak era at Braves Field, but there were a few memorable moments of glory, including the time Tony Cuccinello, Max West and Elbie Fletcher hit consecutive home runs on four pitches from the Giants' powerhouse pitcher Carl Hubbell. Another time, Gene Moore, Buck Jordan and Tony Cuccinello each hit doubles (both times at bat) during an inning against the Cardinals. And who can forget Rabbit Marranville fouling off fourteen straight pitches against the Cubs to extend the inning beyond curfew, causing the score to revert back to the previous inning and giving the Braves the win?

In 1936, Braves Field hosted the All-Star Game. Unfortunately, a miscommunication between the front office and the press resulted in decreased attendance. Due to the erroneous reports that the game was sold out, five thousand seats went unfilled. On the field that day were

Babe Ruth and Wally Berger. *Courtesy of NBHOF.*

Aerial view of Braves Field. *Courtesy of author's collection.*

Lou Gehrig, Jimmie Fox and Joe DiMaggio, who was the 1936 Rookie of the Year.

In 1938, "The Old Professor" Casey Stengel came to Beantown to manage the Braves. Stengel managed the team for six seasons from 1938 to 1943. Stengel tried everything to make the team a winner, but his teams never finished higher than fifth and finished seventh four times. During this time, the park's name changed from Braves Field to National League Park. The club also managed to weather a name change to the Boston Bees. This change lasted from 1936 until 1941, when they reverted back to the Braves.

In addition to Casey taking over the managerial reins, 1938 also saw an overzealous rookie come up to the Braves from San Francisco. The rookie was Vince DiMaggio, older brother of Joe and Dom DiMaggio. Vince could field, throw and hit (when he hit). While Joe DiMaggio set many American League records for hitting, his eldest brother Vince led the National League in strikeouts for six straight years—still a league record. Vince's 134 strikeouts in 1938 are still the most ever by a Brave. Cardinal great Dizzy Dean was so confident he could strike out Vince that he bet a friend he would do so every time he came to bat one game. Dean struck out DiMaggio the first three times he came to the plate, but during his last at-bat in the bottom of the ninth, Vince popped up behind the plate. When Cardinal catcher Booth Ogrodowski settled under the ball for the easy out near, Dean charged from

Vince DiMaggio and Wally Berger. *Courtesy of BPL.*

Casey Stengel and Jim Turner against the backstop wall at Braves Field. *Courtesy of BPL.*

the mound yelling, "Drop it!" Ogrodowski moved out of the way, and Dean caught the ball, thus retiring DiMaggio a fourth time.

During Stengel's stay in Boston, he was accidentally struck by a car in Kenmore Square on a foggy, rainy night during the wartime blackout. Stengel's right leg bones were shattered, and there was talk of amputation. He remained hospitalized for two months at St. Elizabeth's in Brighton, Massachusetts. Boston columnist Dave Egan had little sympathy, though, as he suggested that the motorist who struck Casey be honored as "the man who has done the most for Boston baseball in 1943." Frankie Frisch couldn't resist ribbing Casey about his accident either. He sent his get-well wishes to Casey c/o the psychiatric ward.

During Stengel's six-year reign, one of the most memorable players in the dugout was Max West, a lefty power hitter with no fielding ability but a "Charlie Hustle" on the field. In 1941, the Bees were hosting the Phillies in a fight for the basement. West was thrown out at first and returning to the dugout on the third base line. When he crossed behind the plate, the ball rolled past his feet. West thought it was foul, so he picked it up and tossed it to Phillies catcher Mickey Livingston. West watched in shame as Livingston tagged out the Bees runner trying to score on the passed ball. Stengel, with red face, blasted West in the dugout. West went to the water cooler, and just as he bent over to drink, Paul Waner drove a foul into the dugout, smashing West in the mouth and sending him to the hospital. Max West will probably best be remembered for the three times he was called out for over sliding a base and then for not sliding far enough. He constantly lost fly balls in the sun and tried to challenge his strength against the outfield fence. One time this resulted in splitting his head open. As they carted West past Stengel, Stengel noted, "You've got a great pair of hands, Max."

In 1942, the Braves were starting to rebuild, slowly, of course. The start of the rebuilding process was a weak-armed outfielder named Tommy Holmes who could really hit the ball. Equally impressive that year was a Tobin batting frenzy at Braves Field. In one of the greatest swatting fests ever by a Major League pitcher, Tobin nailed four home runs in five at-bats. This came after a pinch-hit home run just the day before. Tobin also hit three home runs on May 13, 1942, to win his own game 6–5.

Paul Waner also had a big year in 1942. He got his 3,000th hit after turning one chance down. Waner hit a grounder to Cincinnati infielder Eddie Joost, who juggled it briefly before throwing too late to get Waner out. Waner signaled toward the press box so that they wouldn't count this hit. He wanted number three thousand to be a legitimate hit, and scorekeeper Gerry Moore

Max West injured while sliding into home. *Courtesy of George Altison.*

obliged by ruling an error on Joost's throw. Two days later, Waner tapped Pittsburgh's Rip Sewell for a solid and legitimate single.

Generally speaking, Braves Field and the Braves ball club were considered the National League's Devil's Island. This club was where washed-up has-beens and unproven rookies either sat out their days until retirement or waited to be picked up by a better team. John McGraw told two players he sold to the Braves in 1942, "You're going down the river, you're headed for Boston." For years after that statement, countless statistics supported McGraw's opinion, but in the early 1940s, any careful observer could see that was about to change.

In 1945, Tommy Holmes set the modern-day National League record by hitting safely in thirty-seven straight games. In a July double-header at Braves Field against the Pirates, Holmes tied and then broke Roger Hornsby's thirty-three-game mark. Holmes hit .352 that season, striking out only nine times. He was only three points shy of the batting title, which was won by Cub Phil Cavarretta.

The most memorable Opening Day was in 1946, when the Braves converted a potential public relations disaster into $1 million worth of publicity. Approximately 5,000 of the 18,261 who attended the Opening Day game went home wearing green paint on their clothes (the paint had not yet dried on the seats in the grandstand).

Above: Casey Stengel arguing with an umpire at Braves Field in 1941. *Courtesy of George Altison.*

Top: Umpire arguing with Pirates manager Frankie Frisch at Braves Field. *Courtesy of BPL.*

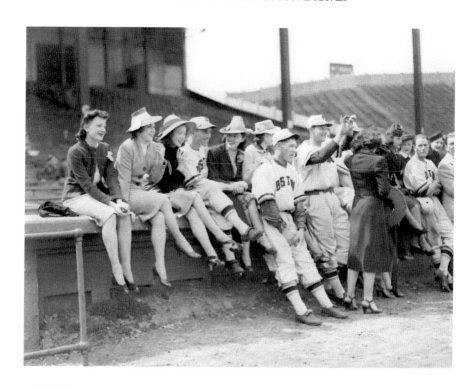

Above: Tommy Holmes and first baseman Joe McCarthy enjoy some down time during 1941 spring training at Choate School in Wallingford, Connecticut. *Courtesy of George Altison.*

Opposite, top: Players and wives relaxing after a game at Braves Field circa 1939. *From left to right*: Ralph Hodges, Buddy Hassett and Max West. *Courtesy of BPL.*

Opposite, bottom: Trolleys line up near Braves Field shortly before a game ends, ready to usher patrons back home. *Courtesy of author's collection.*

The Braves ran full-page ads in Boston newspapers apologizing for the incident and offering to pay the clothing bills. Some thirteen thousand claims poured in, and the Braves paid out about $6,500 to $7,000. It was well worth the publicity to help launch goodwill, and it gave the Braves a new look for the postwar era.

In 1946, the Braves were purchased by Lou Perini, Joe Maney and Guido Rugo. They were local contractors whom the press nicknamed "the three little steam shovels." These owners are hailed by old-time fans as having been the only owners in Braves history to give the fans good baseball and innovative fun at the ballpark. When these owners bought the club, they helped to usher in the Braves' all-too-brief golden period. First they had the lights installed at the field. Then they added TV sets at the concession stands, skyboxes (before they were popular) and the first of baseball's big scoreboards. (Walker Cooper shorted out the scoreboard one night by nailing a home run against it high above the left field fence.) They were also the first owners to have the games televised.

This was also the year that the team departed the National League's second division for the first time in twelve years.

The classic tomahawk uniform was introduced this same year to give the team a new look. The new owners also made the proverbial "offer too good to refuse" to the Cardinals' pennant-winning manager, Billy Southworth, luring him to Boston.

Billy Sullivan kicked the public relations department into high gear with the making of a promotional film, *Take Me Out to the Wigwam*. He also helped publish the first Braves sketchbooks and yearbooks and conducted many promotional activities. The owners thought that scheduling buses for fans who lived in other towns might help to boost attendance. Cape Cod fans were even given the chance to fly to selected games at a cost of fifteen dollars per customer. Braves Field now featured a multicolored grandstand, roof banners, music, fireworks, fight broadcasts and tribal troubadours who roamed the stands. Hedges and evergreens were planted inside the entrance to greet fans, and oversized player photographs hung under the stands.

In May, the tribe played night baseball for the first time in Boston. The foul poles were painted neon to help the umpires, and the team sported a satin version of the tomahawk uniform, which was worn only in night games.

The team finished fourth that year, one game behind the Cubs. They batted .246—a point less than the World Champion Cardinals. Mort Cooper, Johnny Hopp and Phil Masi represented the club in the All-Star Game at Fenway Park. Hopp split his time that year between center field and first base and finished with a batting average of .333, second only in the National League to Stan Musial. In August, Lou Perini agreed to acquire the American Association's Milwaukee Brewers. He predicted that Milwaukee would eventually enter the Major Leagues, which makes one wonder if Perini didn't already have his mind made up about moving the team prior to 1953.

In April 1947, Dodger great Jackie Robinson made his Boston debut at Braves Field despite a slew of death threats.

The mound artistry of Warren Spahn and Johnny Sain accounted for 42 of the Braves' 86 wins in the 1947 season and helped the team finish a respectable third. Die-hard Braves fans still remember the cry, "Spahn and Sain and pray for rain." They were part of a top-notch pitching staff that led Boston to its second National League pennant in thirty-four years.

The attendance that year reached its highest in Braves history at 1.5 million. Prior to the 1948 season, third baseman Bob Elliott won the National League MVP Award. He was the only player in Boston Braves history to win this

A close play at second base at Braves Field. *Courtesy of author's collection.*

The night game is over and fans are making their way out of the ballpark. View of the park from the right field pavilion. *Courtesy of author's collection.*

Crowds entering through the main gate on Gaffney Street. *Courtesy of author's collection.*

award. Opening Day in 1948 at Braves Field unveiled more improvements to the park. The most noticeable was the new scoreboard, which rose sixty-eight feet in the outfield and cost the franchise $70,000. This scoreboard was a predecessor for the modern Jumbotron scoreboards we see today.

The next year brought the best return ever. Bob Elliott smashed a home run on September 27, 1948, clinching the team's first pennant since 1914. More than a million Boston fans cheered for Spahn, Sain and a rookie from LSU named Alvin Dark. Dark went on to win Rookie of the Year that season.

Cleveland's Indians were to provide the competition for the Braves. This would prove to be an exciting but disappointing World Series for the Braves fans. The series opener was a classic pitching duel between Boston's Sain and Cleveland's ace, Bob Feller. Feller, who had waited ten years to pitch in a series, allowed only two hits but lost on a play Cleveland fans still are protesting. The count was two and two in the bottom of the eighth, and Feller had apparently picked off Phil Masi at second, but umpire Bill Stewart ruled Masi safe.

Warren Spahn (21) backing up catcher Phil Masi during the 1948 World Series at Braves Field. *Courtesy of author's collection.*

After Feller protested, Holmes singled and Masi scored the game's only run, putting the Braves ahead by one game. Spahn started game two but was pulled in the fifth inning and wound up a loser in a 4–1 game. After two games in Boston, the teams headed to Cleveland for game three. The Braves sent out Vern Bickford to face Gene Bearden, the twenty-seven-year-old freshman who had suffered serious injuries in the war. Both sides got the same number of hits, but the Indians used their five to score two runs while the Braves went scoreless against Bearden. The next day, the Indians again got five hits off Sain and strung them together for a 2–1 victory.

The Indians now had three straight wins since dropping the series opener to Boston. Cleveland sent out Feller to clinch the title in game five, but the Braves weren't going down easy. They got a hold of Feller's fastball and knocked him out of the box in the seventh inning while rolling on to an 11–5 victory. The victory may have given Boston false hope, because in game six

Main entrance of Braves Field. *Courtesy of author's collection.*

the Indians really turned up the heat, jumping out to a 4–1 lead after the seventh inning. In the bottom of the ninth, the Braves loaded the bases with one out, and Cleveland brought out Bearden to put out the fire. One run scored on a sacrifice fly and another on a pinch double by Masi, but Bearden kept the tying run on third to win the game and end the series.

After the World Series loss in 1948, attendance again dropped and so did the on-field product. In 1949 the team slipped into fourth place. It was Eddie Stanky's last season with Boston and Del Crandall's first.

In 1950, the Braves brought Sam Jethroe to the club. Jethroe has the distinction of being the first black man to wear a Boston uniform. He was a fair singles hitter and a less-than-fair outfielder. He was also the only player to be hit on the head at Braves Field. This incident occurred during a 1952 preseason game between the Red Sox and the Braves when Red Soxer Vern Stephens hit a fly ball into the outfield.

On August 29, 1951, Johnny Sain was traded to New York in return for $50,000 and Selva Lewis Burdette. Tommy Holmes replaced Billy Southworth as manager in midseason as Boston recorded a fourth-place finish for the third time. Charlie Grimm, who replaced Holmes as manager

Boston Brave first baseman Earl Torgeson amazes fans by diving atop the Cleveland dugout to catch a foul ball during a 1948 World Series game at Braves Field. *Courtesy of author's collection.*

Sam "Jet" Jethroe thrown out at third base at Braves Field in 1950. *Courtesy of NBHOF.*

in 1952, was quoted as saying, "We were playing to the grounds help." The fans felt that the team's best years were behind them. In 1952 the last Major League game was played at Braves Field in front of 8,822 fans. The Braves lost to Brooklyn that fateful day with a score of 8–2. The Boston ball club lost half a million dollars that year, and the team finished in seventh place, the lowest in a decade.

Several weeks after the 1952 season, Lou Perini held a top secret meeting with Braves' front office staff at his construction company's offices in Framingham, Massachusetts. Present at the meeting on that gloomy October day were general manager John Quinn, business manager Joe Cairnes and administrative assistant Chuck Patterson. The meeting was held twenty miles outside of Boston because Perini was afraid word would leak out if they held it at the club's front office. Perini began the meeting by outlining that from 1948 to 1952 the franchise had suffered a devastating 80 percent drop in attendance. They also lost $1 million from 1950 to 1952. Patterson recalled, "He told us the Braves couldn't be competitive in Boston, based on market surveys and that the future there was bleak. Then he told us not to say a word to anyone, not even our wives. We're moving to Milwaukee." Over the next few months, Perini entered into private negotiations with civic officials from Milwaukee, who were breaking new ground by using tax dollars to build a new stadium in an attempt to lure a big league team to the area. Bill

Lou Perini—the man who moved the Braves out of Boston. *Courtesy of NBHOF.*

Veeck was very interested in moving his ball team there. However, because the Braves owned the minor league Brewers, Perini would have to relinquish territorial rights to the area, which he wouldn't do—even for $500,000 that Veeck offered. On March 13, 1953, the *Sporting News* broke the story that the Braves were contemplating a move to Milwaukee. Eddie Mathews recalled Perini's answer when questioned by a Milwaukee reporter: "His answer was, 'I can't confirm it, and I can't unconfirm it.' When he didn't deny it everybody knew it was true."

Boston fans believed that Perini would never leave his hometown with their team—this would be heresy. They figured Perini was doing this as a ploy to possibly get more money out of Veeck or possibly some player trade deal.

On the morning of March 18, 1953, at the Vinoy Park Hotel in St. Petersburg, Florida, the National League owners convened behind closed doors to decide the Braves' fate. The meeting lasted only three and a half hours. Once it was over, President Giles emerged to announce that they had unanimously approved the relocation of the team. Their reason was that they believed the move represented an economic opportunity for the entire National League, since the team owners shared gate revenues.

Just weeks before the start of the 1953 season, Braves owner Lou Perini announced that plans had been finalized to move the team to Milwaukee. The move was unexpected because no Major League team had moved since

1900. Even the Braves players were taken by surprise, as they and their families were getting ready to head to Boston when word was sent. Most of them learned of the move during spring training, when several boxes of hats were brought out and passed out among the players. The hats had an *M* on them instead of a *B*. After Perini moved the ball club to Milwaukee, other financially troubled teams began considering moving as an option. These teams were the Dodgers who moved in 1957, the Senators in 1960, the Giants in 1957, the Athletics in 1954 and, last but not least, the St. Louis Browns in 1953. Lou Perini probably didn't realize it in 1953, but by moving the Braves he changed the face of Major League Baseball forever. If Perini had kept the Braves in Boston, it is my belief that the Braves would have been more popular than the Red Sox.

Warren Spahn was probably the most surprised by the decision to move the team. He had invested heavily in a diner on Commonwealth Avenue across from Babcock Street. The diner was to bear his name and had the slogan "The best in baseball—The best in food." The opening of the diner was to coincide with Opening Day at Braves Field in 1953. The diner was expecting to get a lot of the business from the ballpark as well as crowds that would be attending the 1953 All-Star Game (which was rescheduled to be played elsewhere). Spahn eventually sold out his interest in the diner, which transitioned into a Hayes-Bickford and, ultimately, a muffler shop.

Perini did attempt to keep the team in Boston when he had a secretive meeting with Red Sox owner Tom Yawkey. He requested that Yawkey allow the Braves to play at Fenway while Braves Field was remodeled and updated. Yawkey refused, and Perini had to seek other options. Yawkey wanted Boston to become a one-team town so he could have a monopoly on baseball and gate revenue in the city. Yawkey's greed ruined Boston and ended almost sixty years of the city being a two-team town. Fact is that Boston supported its two teams better than Chicago had. Perini bought a team that had suffered from financial problems since its conception. When Perini bought the club, he immediately started renovating the aging park. These renovations were necessary to help modernize the park. Yawkey did the same thing when he bought the Red Sox and Fenway Park. Perini didn't have the money that Yawkey had and only performed necessary repairs to the park. Perini had plans drawn up in 1950 that would bring the park into the modern baseball era. He knew television would become the main revenue stream for baseball and that amenities such as luxury boxes would help increase revenue. The majority of National League owners still viewed gate receipts as the main source of income. Perini was also the first owner to move into a park that was taxpayer funded.

Braves Field

Spahn's Diner on Commonwealth Avenue. *Courtesy of BU Archives.*

The Boston Braves were like no other ball club back then—or now. This club treated its fans like family. They had fan appreciation days and raffles for automobiles. Braves Field was the only ballpark in Major League history to serve fried clams at the concession stands. Many fans probably remember the feeling of awe they felt when they would walk up the main ramp to the grandstand. The people who worked at Braves Field were friendlier than the workers at Fenway Park. Braves Field had a more welcoming atmosphere than any park before or since.

To this day, it still saddens me that the Braves are gone. But I'm happy to say that if you do go to Boston University's Nickerson Field, there are still many reminders that National League ball was played here. A plaque was placed on this site in 1988 during a Braves player reunion. Old-time Braves fans are still fiercely loyal, even though the team has been gone for over fifty years. They will never let it be forgotten that the Braves originated in Boston. To the loyal, the Atlanta Braves are not America's team; that title belongs to the Boston Braves. The Braves truly were Boston's team. Only the Brooklyn fans rivaled their fans' loyalty. Boston Braves fans did not and would not transfer their loyalty to Milwaukee.

Braves Field had its own distinct personality that made it different than any park in the Majors. Casey Stengel used to refer to the wind that blew off

The Braves' all-rookie infield of 1952. These men were the heart of the 1957 Milwaukee Braves World Series team. *From left to right*: George Crowe, Jack Dittmar, Johnny Logan and Eddie Mathews. *Courtesy of author's collection.*

Abandoned Braves Field in 1953. *Courtesy of author's collection.*

Abandoned outfield. Notice the Jury Box. *Courtesy of author's collection.*

the Charles River as "Old Joe Wind, my fourth outfielder." When Boston batters would complain about the outfield gusts, Casey would reply, "You know Roger Hornsby played here and hit .387 in that wind."

An interesting sidenote: in 1953, under the cover of darkness, several loyal fans broke into the ballpark. They immediately headed over to home plate, dug down several feet by hand and stole home plate. Almost fifty years later, the culprits donated the item to the Sports Museum of New England, and all was forgiven.

After the Braves abandoned Braves Field before the 1953 season, it was purchased by Boston University. Some historians have said that the university purchased the field for $50,000, which was the tax money owed. Other historians have stated that the old ballpark was purchased for $430,000; either way it was a major coup for Boston University and its athletic program.

In 1954, Boston University took over the park to get it ready for the start of the 1954 football season. The first changes were made at the end of the season when the original outfield wall came down. In September 1955,

View from the right field pavilion looking toward where home plate once was. Notice how the dormitories were built on the footprint of the old grandstand. *Courtesy of author's collection.*

demolition began on the Jury Box and, in October, the third base pavilion. The park remained this way until 1959, when demolition was begun on the grandstand seating after the Syracuse game. What remained then was the clubhouse, which would be used for the next five years by Boston University's football team. In fact, former Boston Braves PR man Billy Sullivan, who was the owner of the Boston (now New England) Patriots, called the old park home from 1960 to 1962.

It is truly a shame that Boston University didn't make more of an attempt to preserve the past. I was informed by Ralph Evans, who is a well-known expert on Braves Field, that if Boston University had not been so eager to modernize its newly acquired field and had just considered preserving the past, the field may have been able to remain virtually untouched.

The right field pavilion and the main entrance on Gaffney Street are all that remain of the original ballpark. Boston University laid a football carpet in front of the right field pavilion. The main entrance is now occupied by the Boston University Police Department. Part of the original concrete outfield

This plaque was placed behind the former main entrance of Braves Field in 1988. The plaque formally recognizes the historic significance of the site and helps to keep the history of Braves Field preserved for future generations. *Courtesy of author's collection.*

Removal of the left field pavilion began in 1954. *Courtesy of BU Archives.*

View of main entrance and right field pavilion on Gaffney Street. *Courtesy of author's collection.*

wall still stands, as do the fir trees that the owners planted in the 1940s to help hide the railroad yard behind the old outfield.

The scoreboard was sold in 1955 for $100,000 and was placed in right center field in the refurbished, newly named Municipal Stadium in Kansas City, Missouri—the home of the Kansas City Athletics from 1955 to 1967 and the Kansas City Royals from 1969 to 1972. In a Rhode Island softball stadium, fans sit on Braves Field seats. These seats are now highly priced and prized among many collectors.

Boston Braves baseball is gone forever and so are the fans' hopes that the Braves will return, or at least that Major League Baseball will flourish again in Braves Field.

CHAPTER 5
INTERESTING PLAYER STORIES

Los Angeles Times columnist Mike Downey called the Braves "the team that is to Major League Baseball what Gomer Pyle was to the U.S. Marines." As humorous as that statement might be, I'm sure once you finish reading this chapter you'll also see how profound it is.

Aside from the Braves being the only franchise in modern Major League Baseball to have fielded a team every season of professional league play, they also had some tragic and funny events happen to their players. I felt that these short stories needed to be in this book. However odd they may be, they help us get an overall picture of the legacy of National League baseball in Boston.

In 1894, catcher Charlie Bennett lost both legs when he slipped under the wheels of a moving train while trying to board. A benefit game was held for him in 1894 at the Congress Street Grounds. Heavyweight boxing champ "Gentleman" Jim Corbett played several innings. The $6,000 in receipts was given to Bennett, who used the money to open a pottery in Detroit. He was so well thought of in Detroit that the first American League field was named after him. He lived to be seventy-two.

Most people think O.J. Simpson was the first athlete turned killer, but really it was Braves catcher Marty Bergen. In 1900, Bergen killed his wife, two young children and himself using an axe and a razor.

Francis Quimlet was elected vice-president of the Braves in 1941. He made sporting history in 1913 when he won the U.S. Open as an amateur at the age of nineteen. Coincidentally, he used to play golf at the Allston Golf Links before Gaffney purchased the site for Braves Field.

The Braves' spring training was held in Miami in 1916. When the team broke camp, they headed back north by train and played exhibition games on the way to help pay expenses. This practice was considered standard in the early days of baseball. But Walter Hapgood, the Braves' business manager, scheduled so many games that the players had to sleep on trains for twenty straight nights. After a week the players decided that if they were going to be treated like hobos then they'd look like them too. They stopped shaving and began wearing gaudy ties and work shirts. A store owner in Georgia called the sheriff to report the presence of jailbreakers in town. Hapgood quickly got the message and changed the schedule.

There have been only a handful of triple plays in modern Major League history. The only one in Braves history occurred on October 6, 1923. It was the first in the National League since 1878. The play was made by Ernie "Red" Padgett, a twenty-four-year-old shortstop who was appearing in just his second game in the Major Leagues. The Braves were playing at home in a double-header against Philadelphia. In the fourth inning, Philadelphia had Cliff Lee at first base and Cotton Tierney at second with no outs. Walter Holke hit a line drive at Padgett, who caught the ball, touched second to get Tierney out and tagged the unsuspecting Lee between first and second. Boston won the game, which was shortened to four and a half innings due to darkness, by a score of 4–1. Padgett's career never amounted to much, but this play makes him a standout.

Tony Boekel, a third baseman who once drove in the only run in a twenty-six-inning game, lost his life in an auto accident in 1924.

Player/manager Dave Bancroft was once leveled by a punch from Pittsburgh catcher Earl Smith as he was crossing the plate in 1927.

On January 10, 1930, two professional ballplayers squared off in public for profit for the first and only time in history. Seventeen thousand people paid to see Braves catcher Al Spohrer box White Sox first baseman Art Shires at the Boston Garden. Shires stood six feet, one inch and weighed 195 pounds. Spohrer stood five feet, ten inches and weighed 175 pounds. Spohrer went down in the second round until the count of nine. He was able to get back up and rally for a short while. In the fourth round, Spohrer's friend threw the towel in for him since Spohrer was still in a daze from the pounding. As luck would have it, Shires came to the Braves in 1932.

Al Montgomery, a catcher for the 1941 Braves, appeared in the movie *Pride of the Yankees* as the masked catcher for several teams. He was killed in an auto accident in 1942 at the age of twenty-one.

The Braves were one of the last teams to install lights. When they finally did on May 11, 1946, a crowd of 37,407 (the largest at Braves Field in thirteen years) turned out. The crowd witnessed baseball history but also saw the Braves lose to the Giants 5–1. The team was sporting brand-new night game jerseys with red piping. These uniforms were supposed to reflect the artificial light that was produced by the stadium lights. They never really caught on with the players or the fans.

In the movie *The Natural*, starring Robert Redford, another former Brave had a brief acting career as the opposing manager. He was Sibby Sisti.

Jeff Heath, an outfielder with the 1948 team, is also in the Canadian Baseball Hall of Fame.

In 1949, Connie Ryan was the victim of the most unusual ejection in baseball history. He was thrown out of a game for wearing a raincoat while in the on-deck circle. He was protesting against the soggy playing conditions.

Bill Voiselle was the only Major League player to wear the name of his hometown on his uniform. Voiselle, who came from Ninety Six, South Carolina, wore the number 96.

Phil Paine, a pitcher for the Braves in 1951, also became the first Major Leaguer to play in Japan. In 1953 Paine was stationed in Japan with the U.S. Air Force. It was there that he pitched for the Nishitetsu Lions.

Waldon Williams was the first African American player to sign with the team. He signed in December 1948 but never made it out of the farm team.

Sam "Jet" Jethroe has the distinction of being the Braves' first African American player.

Although the date is unknown, baseball lore has it that the longest home run was hit by a Brave at the Congress Street Grounds. The park was adjacent to Boston Harbor. Legend has it that the ball was hit out of the park, landed on an Australian-bound freighter and traveled halfway across the country.

Fred Browne, an outfielder for the Beaneaters from 1901 to 1902, was elected governor of New Hampshire in 1913. He later served as a U.S. senator from 1933 to 1939 and then was appointed comptroller general of the United States.

The smallest man to ever play for the Braves was Walter "Punk" or "Doc" Gautreau. A second baseman from 1925 to 1928, he stood five feet, four inches and weighed 129 pounds. In 1927, he stole home twice in one game to tie a Major League record.

Reserve catcher Frank Gibson is best known for the most unusual holdout in baseball history. He held out one spring not for more money but rather more work.

Whitey Wietelmann, Braves infielder from 1939 to 1946, was pitching batting practice when the little finger on his left hand was shattered. This incident caused him to have part of his finger amputated.

Ebbets Field had its "Sym-Phony" band, and Braves Field was no different. Here we see the Braves Field Troubadours in 1948. These merry men would walk around the park playing songs to entertain the crowd. *Courtesy of BPL.*

When the spitball was outlawed in 1920, only eight pitchers were allowed to continue throwing it. One of them was Braves pitcher Dana Fillingim.

Walt Cruise, who scored the only run in the twenty-six-inning game of 1920, was married between games during a double-header in Cincinnati. He did not play in the second game.

Shanty Hogan, who played catcher for the Braves for two seasons, missed three days of spring training in 1933 because of a sunburn. Later that year he had a string of 121 errorless games behind the plate that extended into 1934.

The Braves acquired Yankee great Lefty Gomez after the 1942 season. He attended spring training with the Braves in 1943 and was carried on the roster in April but never pitched.

Lefthander Patsy Flaherty, who pitched for Boston from 1907 to 1908 and in 1911, was so good at quick pitching batters that he's given much of the credit for the rule against the practice.

Pirates' pitcher Guy Bush, who gave up home runs 713 and 714 to Babe Ruth (then with the Braves) in 1935, became a Brave the following year.

Hod Ford was still a student at Tufts University in 1919 when he became a Braves infielder.

Pat "Doc" Carney's career lasted for only four years (all with Boston) from 1901 to 1904. After trying his hand at both pitching and fielding, he decided his career opportunities were elsewhere. He returned to his alma mater, Holy Cross, and coached baseball for four years before becoming a physician.

Braves pitcher Bunny Hearn coached baseball at the University of North Carolina for twenty-seven years.

Al Demaree's pitching career came to a close in 1919. He then became a syndicated sports cartoonist whose work appeared in the *Sporting News* for over thirty years.

Former Braves manager Charlie Grimm had his ashes scattered over Wrigley Field when he died at age eighty-five.

Mort Cooper used to chew aspirin while he was on the mound to relieve a sore arm.

Roy Hartsfield, who played for the Braves from 1950 to 1952, became the first manager of the expansion team the Toronto Blue Jays in 1977.

Braves shortstop Doc Farrell was a dentist in the offseason.

Les Mann, an outfielder for the 1914 Miracle Braves, promoted baseball after his playing career. Commissioner Landis called him the "Ambassador of American Baseball."

Some of the toughest Major League players of all time wore Boston Braves uniforms. Even though Johnny Logan stood only five feet, ten inches, he never backed down from a fight—he never lost one, either. One time he even took on Don Drysdale. Eddie Mathews trained in martial arts as a youngster. He once beat up Frank Robinson between games of a double-header. He also knocked out Don Drysdale with one punch after Drysdale threw a pitch at his head. Pete Whisehant is widely considered baseball's all-time tough guy. He once knocked out Paul Miner with one punch (breaking Miner's neck in the process) at an after-hours nightspot. In fact, while he was with the Braves he returned to his locker after the game only to find his clothes nailed above his locker. This was something the veterans used to do to initiate the newcomers. The next day, Pete collected all of the clothes from the lockers of the half dozen or so offenders—including Warren Spahn. He then piled their clothes in the shower and turned it on. As the players entered the shower room to salvage their clothing, he announced, "If any #%@! wants to #%$@ with my things again they can take it up with me right here, right now!" Needless to say they didn't bother him again.

During the spring of 1953, Sibby Sisti and Warren Spahn were filming a commercial for Gillette in St. Petersburg, Florida. Sisti had just finished

Braves players exhibiting the year 1948. *Courtesy of NBHOF.*

his portion of the commercial and was leaving the set when he came across a ticker tape machine. The breaking story on the machine was about the Braves' sudden move to Milwaukee. Sibby ran back to the set to inform Spahn and the director. The director, rather than shooting the commercial over again, advised the announcer to describe Spahn as formerly with the Boston Braves and now with the Milwaukee Braves. That is how two of the biggest stars on the team found out about the move.

Warren Spahn bought two beach cottages on Anna Marie Island in Florida for his family and friends to stay at while he was in spring training. He aptly named the cottages The Infield and The Outfield. He then built the only two-story cottage in the area and named it The Diamond. He eventually added four more, naming them The Mound, Home Plate, Catcher's Mitt and Shortstop. This baseball compound housed many of Spahn's teammates and friends over the years. Once his career in baseball was over, Spahn sold off many of the properties, only retaining The Infield for his family. Two of the cottages have been torn down, and Spahn's son donated the other 832-square-foot bungalow to the Anna Maria Island Historical Society. The cottage is going to be moved onto the museum property and will show the baseball history of the area in an exhibit entitled "The Boys of Winter."

I hope now that everybody realizes why these stories in varying degrees are indispensable pieces of Boston baseball history.

CHAPTER 6

BRAVES MANAGERS

Besides the antics of the players and the front office, there is one other group that needs mention—the managers.

Many of the managers failed, but a few succeeded, and these men helped compose a rich and entertaining chapter in Boston baseball.

From 1876 to 1881, Harry Wright reigned as manager of the Braves. Wright's contributions to baseball are numerous. He is often referred to as a "baseball Edison." He introduced pregame batting practice and originated team play by teaching his players to back each other up on defense. He was also the first manager to use hand signals to direct his players. Wright's managerial career percentage is .581 in Boston. Wright managed the Phillies after Boston and officially retired in 1893. Because of his stature in the game, he was named the National League's first supervisor of umpires. Three years later he died at the age of sixty.

When the Red Stockings' owners decided to replace Wright, they chose John Morrill. Morrill was not only one of the most popular players ever to wear a Boston uniform, but he was also a hometown product who established himself as a reliable and dependable player with the club. Morrill was able to get the club back into contention with a third-place finish in 1882. Then, in 1883, Morrill executed one of the strangest managerial moves in the Boston club's history—he turned the managerial position over to second baseman Jack Burdock. On July 23, the team found itself in fourth place, so Morrill regained control as manager and led the club to its first pennant since 1878. After 1884 it was all downhill, and in 1888 Morrill was sold to Washington.

He later retired from baseball and became a sporting goods dealer and a sportswriter for the *Boston Journal*.

An interesting point about Jack Burdock's managerial career, which lasted just fifty-four games in 1883, was that he was replaced because he embarrassed the club (and the league) by grabbing the opposing catcher during a game to prevent him from catching a foul pop-up. The umpire fined him twenty dollars on the spot. Burdock played fourteen seasons in the National League but never managed again.

Even though Morrill was the manager during the 1887 season, he had little control of the team because in the early days of baseball, the team's captain often was more powerful than the manager. Boston's team captain was King Kelly. Under Kelly, the team languished in fifth place and lacked direction, so Morrill regained control for the final month of the 1887 season.

In 1889, Boston got a new manager by the name of Jim Hart. Although he brought the club just one game out of first, he still lost his job. His .648 winning percentage is the best in franchise history for a one-season manager. Hart was a conservative man who was content to let Kelly take center stage. This complacent attitude was one of the factors that led to his demise as manager. On October 2, the next-to-last day of the season, Boston suffered a loss to Cleveland. This defeat was particularly devastating as Kelly was unable to play because he showed up drunk. Hart was blamed for Kelly's drunkenness and became the scapegoat for Boston not winning the pennant. Though Hart never managed again, he did just fine. He went to Chicago and became president of the Cubs in 1891.

In 1890, Frank Selee became manager. In his twelve-year tenure from 1890 to 1901, he won five pennants—all between 1891 and 1898. He holds franchise records for pennants, games (1,677), wins (1,004), full seasons (12) and winning percentage (.607) for managers with more than one year of service. Selee wasn't a brilliant strategist, but he was an absolute master at building a team and recognizing talent. He always made sure that he had the best-prepared players in the game. His players were mentally, physically and fundamentally sound and were known for outthinking their opponents. In twelve years with Boston, Selee had ten first-division teams and five pennant winners. He won nearly 61 percent of his games. He never made more than $3,500 a year, but he did supplement his income with ownership of a haberdashery. When Boston cut Selee loose, he was picked up by the Cubs. It was in Chicago that he truly made his mark in baseball history by assembling the famed infield of Tinker, Evers and Chance. In 1909, he died from tuberculosis at the age of forty-nine. Selee was the greatest manager in Braves history.

Arthur Soden hired Al Buckenberger as Selee's replacement in 1902. He arrived in Boston at a crucial time, one that would lead to the first extended period of pathetic baseball in Boston history. To his credit, he coaxed the team into third place, getting the Braves nine games over .500 in 1902. The next two seasons were disastrous, and Buckenberger was fired in 1904 after the team finished fifty-one games out of first. The Braves would never dig themselves out of the hole they had fallen into, and Buckenberger would never manage again.

From 1905 to 1907, Fred Tenney reigned as manager. Soden told Tenney that he needn't worry about winning games. He was promised a bonus if he could help them stop losing money. Tenney's best team was the 1907 club, which finished in seventh place. In 1908, the Dovey brothers traded Tenney to New York, but in 1911, yet another owner, William Russell, brought Tenney back to Boston. The 1911 team played to a .291 winning percentage, the second worst showing in Boston history. Tenney was fired at the end of the season even though he had another year remaining on his contract.

From 1908 to 1910, Boston saw four different managers. The first was Joe Kelley. Kelley wasn't known for his managerial skills, but he was known for his vanity. He had an unusual habit of carrying a mirror in his uniform pocket, and it was not uncommon to see him pull it out on the field so he could take a quick look at himself. Kelley got the club up to sixth place in 1908—its best finish since 1903. He was undermined by catcher Frank Bowerman, who also wanted to be manager and was good friends with team president George Dovey. Dovey fired Kelley at the end of the 1908 season and gave the job to Bowerman. Bowerman would only last seventy-six games before he was sent home to rest. (He looked like he was on the verge of a nervous breakdown.) He returned to the team in mid-July and resigned immediately.

Harry Smith took over as manager upon Bowerman's resignation. Smith's record was as horrid as Bowerman's. Boston was in last place when Smith took over and remained there until the season ended. He was not asked to manage again. Another year, another manager.

In 1910, Fred Lake became the team's manager. Of course, a new manager mattered not, because Boston finished at the bottom of the National League again. Lake had another year on his contract, but the club bought it out and brought Tenney back.

Johnny Kling became manager in 1912. Kling came to Boston in a midseason trade in 1911. The following season he became a player/manager. A year later he was gone. Such was the fate of Boston managers in this period.

Then, in 1913, the Braves hired George "Tweedy" Stallings. They were making their eighth managerial change in seven years. Stallings was known as a gentleman off the field. He was anything but that on the field. He was known as abusive, brilliant, profane, temperamental and even superstitious. During Stallings's college days, he was good enough to get a tryout with the Phillies in 1887. Harry Wright was manager of the Phillies then and convinced Stallings to give up school and play baseball. It seems almost profound that Wright had this chance encounter with Stallings in 1887, because in 1914, Stallings would lead the team to its only World Series win in history. Although Stallings didn't invent platooning, he probably perfected it. Without his constant lineup juggling, it's doubtful that the 1914 Braves could have performed their miracle. Stallings was also credited with popularizing the use of right-handed hitters against left-handed pitching and vice versa. Stallings was so superstitious that, just because he ate two slices of lemon pie before a game and the team won, he had the same pregame snack for the next nine days until they lost. He thought peanut shells and loose scraps of paper were bad luck. Cubs infielder Hennie Zimmerman used to tear up scraps of paper and drop them in front of the Boston dugout just to torment Stallings. Although Stallings never repeated the miracle of 1914, he didn't have any horrid years like some of the other managers. In November 1920, Stallings resigned because he was dissatisfied with his contract and the lack of money that was needed to acquire new players. He retired to his six-thousand-acre plantation in Georgia, where he died of heart failure in 1929.

After Stallings resigned, pitching coach Fred Mitchell became manager. Mitchell, a native of Cambridge, Massachusetts, first played for the Braves in 1913. He left in 1916 to coach at Harvard. Mitchell was part Cherokee and a strict disciplinarian. However, by 1923, the team had lost one hundred games for the second season in a row, and Mitchell was let go as manager. He did, however, continue as a scout for the club.

During the 1928 season, Boston saw the rise and fall of two managers. The first was Jack Slattery. Slattery was a Braves coach in 1918 under Stallings but left to coach at local colleges. Then, in 1928, Judge Fuchs requested he manage the Braves. Shortly after Slattery became manager, Fuchs acquired Roger Hornsby in a trade with the Giants. Needless to say, Hornsby and Slattery did not see eye to eye. After a rough road trip of thirty-one games, Slattery resigned from his two-year contract. This paved the way for Hornsby to become manager. As bad as the Braves played under Slattery, they played even worse for Hornsby.

At the end of the 1928 season, Fuchs was offered five players and $200,000 for Hornsby from the Cubs. This offer was too good to refuse for the cash-strapped Fuchs.

Then, in an unprecedented move, Fuchs named himself as manager in 1929, saying, "I don't think our club can do any worse with me as manager than it has done the last few years." Even though Fuchs was the manager, assistant manager Johnny Evers actually had the power. The players didn't pay much attention to Fuchs when he was in the dugout. This only added to the impression that this was not a ball club to be taken seriously. Fuchs's managerial percentage was a pitiful .364.

From 1930 to 1937, Bill McKechnie reigned as manager. Nicknamed "Deacon Bill" because of his churchgoing ways, he managed in the Majors for a quarter of a century. He also played in the Majors for eleven years, including one game for the Braves in 1913. During his big league managerial career, he won four pennants and two World Series titles—unfortunately, not one of these was with Boston. In fact, the only award he received during his stay in Boston came in 1937 when he was named Manager of the Year for leading a very bad Boston team to a winning record of 79 and 73. McKechnie also helped the club financially by passing on an occasional paycheck. In 1937, he left the Braves for a better contract with Cincinnati.

The next manager the Braves had is regarded as one of the greatest managers of all time. Casey Stengel won ten pennants and seven World Series with the New York Yankees. But when he managed Boston from 1938 to 1943, the Braves fans would never have believed that he would be regarded as a great manager later on. The Braves were instrumental in making Stengel a manager. In 1925, Stengel was a player for the Braves before they released him and sent him to Worcester, Massachusetts, to serve as player/manager and club president. Even though the Braves played poorly under Stengel, he was well liked by the players and fans. He even felt comfortable enough to purchase stock in the ailing franchise. During one of Stengel's many ejections, Umpire Bill Klem said to him, "I always suspected you were crazy, but now I'm convinced. I just heard you bought stock in this ball club. No sane man would ever do that."

In 1943, the Perini regime sent Stengel packing, and Braves coach Bob Coleman took the reins. Perini was determined to make the club a contender, but first he would have to wait out the war. From 1943 to 1945, Coleman was looked upon as nothing more than an interim manager. He resigned in late July 1945.

1948 pennant-winning team. *Courtesy of author's collection.*

When Coleman resigned, Del Bissonette was given the task of directing the team through its fifty-nine games. Bissonette had little pressure as manager, but he was responsible for the team.

Billy Southworth took over as manager in 1946, and Bissonette, who'd been a minor league manager for the Braves, went to Pittsburgh as a coach. During thirteen seasons managing the Cardinals and the Braves, Southworth won four pennants and nearly 60 percent of his games. No team he managed finished a season in the second division. The Braves gave Southworth a five-year contract that included a $35,000 base salary as well as a bonus plan—$15,000 for second place and $20,000 for the pennant. With Perini's willingness to buy players, Southworth was able to transform the team into contenders and lead them out of the dark. He instilled discipline and hustle in his players through long, rigid practice sessions. Then, in 1948, it all paid off as the Braves won the pennant by six and a half games over the Cardinals.

After the 1948 season, they were favored to repeat as pennant winners in 1949. Instead, they stumbled all the way to fourth place. Almost as quickly as they came together under Southworth, they began to fall apart. Dissension developed among the veterans as they began to resent Southworth's strict rules. Then, in mid-August, Southworth was sent home to rest because he was feeling distraught. Johnny Cooney took over for the last forty-six games. Cooney, who was never officially named manager, is credited for running the club in official records. But, on June 19, 1951, Southworth found himself and the club in fifth place. He was forced to resign, citing health problems, even though he had a year and a half on his contract. He never managed again.

Billy Southworth welcoming Willard Marshall, Sid Gordon and Buddy Kerr. He traded Al Dark and Eddy Stanky to the Giants for these players. *Courtesy of BPL.*

In 1951, the Braves called up Tommy Holmes, a player/manager for the Braves farm club at Hartford. Unfortunately, he was regarded as "one of the boys" by the players and never could get the proper distance between them. Sadly, Holmes was removed and fired on May 31, 1952. His managerial percentage was an average .469. Boston's loss was New York's gain, as Holmes finished the season as a pinch hitter with the Dodgers. He later managed in the minors for five years before working as a scout for one year and eventually becoming director of the Greater New York Sandlot Baseball Foundation. In 1973, he joined the Mets to work in community relations.

Charlie Grimm was brought up from the Braves' minor league team in Milwaukee to replace Holmes. Grimm's half season in Boston was, for the most part, uneventful. He finished the season with a .432 percentage and remained with the Braves until 1956.

CHAPTER 7
BRAVES OWNERS

Ever since I was a child, I have found myself fascinated with the stories of how people like Rockefeller or Carnegie amassed their fortunes. As I researched the former owners of the Braves, I again found myself fascinated. It was then that I realized that, without these owners working in the shadows of the public eye, this team might never have reached such mythical proportions. The Braves front office has been filled with conspiracy, unethical behavior and wrongdoing.

On January 20, 1871, the first meeting of the club was incorporated with $15,000, and Ivers Whitney Adams was voted in as president.

In 1876, Nathaniel T. Appollonio became the team's first president in National League history. Appollonio was elected president on December 3, 1873, but when the club fell into fourth place in 1876, he sold the franchise to Arthur H. Soden. It is believed that Appollonio sold the club because he couldn't handle his club not coming in first place. Prior to the 1877 season, Arthur Soden, William Conant and James Billings took control of the club. Soden was chosen as president, Billings was voted treasurer and Conant became the secretary. All of these positions were voted on by the majority stockholders.

Soden was born in Framingham, Massachusetts. He served as a hospital steward during the Civil War. Later, he went into the wholesale drug business and then into the roofing business, where he became independently wealthy. In addition to being remembered for instituting the reserve clause, he was also widely known for his frugal behavior. During his tenure, complimentary tickets were nonexistent. Even the players' wives had to pay admission. With the arrival of the American League in Boston, Soden quickly realized that his on-field product and gate receipts couldn't compete. So, after the 1906 season, Soden and Conant, who'd bought out Billings two years earlier, sold the team to George and John Dovey.

The Dovey brothers ran a coalmine before going into the railroad business. They teamed up with John Harris of Pittsburgh and purchased the club for $75,000. Although the Doveys ran the club, the chief investor was John Harris. George became club president, and John was the business manager. On June 19, 1909, George died at the age of forty-eight from a hemorrhage of the lungs while on a train bound for a Cincinnati scouting trip. Brother John succeeded him as president, and then he and Harris sold the team at the end of the 1910 season. During the Dovey brothers' tenure as club owners, they made several improvements to the Congress Street Grounds, and as long as they owned the club, it was nicknamed the "Doves."

In 1911, William Hepburn Russell bought the team with a group of investors. Mr. Russell's only contribution to baseball was that he kept the team in Boston. Ned Hanlon tried to buy the franchise with the full intent of moving it to Baltimore. Thank God that Russell refused the offer. Russell was a New York attorney and boyhood friend of Mark Twain. Russell was fifty-four when he purchased the club and in poor health. He died in November, prompting the sale of the club.

John M. Ward and James Gaffney purchased the club for $177,000 in 1911. Ward was not only a successful New York attorney, but he was also a successful National League pitcher in his early years. At the end of the 1912 season, he sold out to Gaffney, saying, "I'm getting out just in time by the looks of it. This club is driving me bughouse." I guess Ward wasn't used to anything short of a winner.

James Gaffney ran the team from 1912 to 1915 while serving as club president. Gaffney started out as a cop before becoming wealthy as a contractor. He brought many changes as club owner, including renaming the team after a Delaware Indian chief. This same Delaware chief also had another society named in his honor—the Tammany Hall Society, of which Gaffney was a member. Members of this society were referred to as the "Tammany Hall Braves," hence the name change of the ball club to the Braves. Gaffney also changed the Old English *B* on the uniform and replaced it with a profile of an Indian chief. He also hired George Stallings as manager, who was instrumental in the club winning the 1914 World Series. Around this time he also purchased the Allston Golf Course, which was to become the team's home. The property was deemed unsuitable for most building projects because of the cost of filling in the large hollow in the middle. The valley, though, formed a natural amphitheater and a low-cost site to build a ballpark. The tiers of concrete and iron seating were built on the hillside, leaving the playing field seventeen feet below street level. The project required one thousand workers, 750 tons of steel and 8.2 million pounds of cement. The park was hailed as the latest in modern convenience by the *Sporting Life* magazine. This was also the only park that had showers and clubhouses under the grandstand.

Gaffney sold his club in 1916 to Percy D. Haughton, who is probably best known for trying to ban the use of profanity on the team. Stallings quickly broke the ban, since profanity was his middle name. Haughton gained recognition as a football player at Harvard University. After he graduated, he worked two seasons as head coach at Cornell University. By 1918, the club had dropped to seventh place, so Haughton's group sold the club. Haughton returned to his alma mater to reorganize the football program.

George Grant purchased the team in 1919. He was a motion picture executive who started the film industry in Europe. He was also a close friend of Giants' owners Charles Stoneham and John McGraw. He purchased the club for $400,000. It was during Grant's tenure as owner that the farm team rumors began to circulate. The Braves traded Art Nehf to the Giants for $40,000 and four pitchers. Nehf went on to help the Giants to four straight pennants from 1921 to 1924. Loyal Braves fans began to believe the rumors after the Giants acquired Nehf and after it was learned that Stoneham loaned Grant the money to buy the Braves. In 1926, Grant sold the team to Judge Emil E. Fuchs. Fuchs served both as New York City magistrate and deputy attorney general of New York State. Fuchs learned about the inner workings of the front office when he served as attorney for the New York Giants. Up until 1929, Sunday play was banned in Boston. But, thanks to Fuchs's vigorous efforts, Sunday play was legalized. In the end, Fuchs was charged with buying the votes and pleaded no contest. The club was fined $1,000 in Boston Municipal Court. Fuchs was also known for wining and dining the sportswriters who covered the team, calling them his "Board of Directors."

In 1933, the club was still in financial distress. A desperate Fuchs announced a plan to hold dog races at Braves Field in an attempt to raise $79,000 to reimburse Adams so he wouldn't lose control of the club. The league, however, was less than enthusiastic about the whole idea and tried to put the kibosh on the whole plan. James Gaffney's estate still controlled Braves Field and they were planning to go ahead with the dog races. The league, which had no other way out of the dog racing fiasco, decided to loan Fuchs $7,500 and took over the lease on the field, subleasing it to the club at a reduced price. On July 31, the judge forfeited his majority share of the team. Fourteen months later, he filed for bankruptcy.

After the season, the league took temporary control of the team until it was reorganized financially. Fuchs returned to his law practice and paid off his debts of $300,000, which was almost what he had paid for the team.

Bob Quinn never actually owned the club but was hired by Charles Adams as the acting owner. Quinn was no stranger to Boston baseball. He served as president of the Red Sox from 1923 to 1932. He will probably best be remembered for changing the Braves name to the Bees. The name resulted from a contest in which the fans were asked to select a new nickname. He also changed the name of the park to National League Park but urged it be referred to as the Beehive. Quinn, tired of running the ailing franchise, persuaded a few fans to organize a new syndicate to buy the club. He later became director of the Baseball Hall of Fame and Museum for four years.

In 1945, Lou Perini, Joe Maney and Guido Rugo bought the team. Perini quit school in the eleventh grade and started a job in his father's construction company as a laborer. He later turned the company into an international firm with his two brothers. When he became president, Perini made his fortune during World War II building tunnels, airports and ammunition dumps. When the "three steam shovels" bought the club in 1945, it had the smallest farm team system in the league. They then did something completely unconventional by giving Harry Jenkins, the Braves' farm director, his own private plane so he could scout the country for prospects. Perini also updated the lighting system at Braves Field. In 1951, Perini bought out Guido Rugo and Joe Maney. By 1953, he owned all but four of the shares. On March 13, the *Sporting News* broke the news that Perini was moving the team to Milwaukee. The next day, Perini announced his intention, and on March 18, the league approved it. Perini relinquished the presidency in 1957 and sold the team in 1962 to the LaSalle Corporation for $6.2 million.

Now that I've given some insight into the Braves' front office history, it will be easier to see that the front office was as inept at times as the on-field product. It seems strange to me that when a restaurant goes out of business, the public blames the management, but when a ball club loses money and packs up and moves to another town, the public blames the ballplayers. I think it's time that we, as a society, put the blame where it belongs. If we had done this sooner, the Braves might still be in Boston. I feel baseball fans have an obligation to the game to hold the front office officials of any club accountable for their decisions. Ball clubs don't realize that diehard fans are their team's true supporters, not the corporations that buy the skybox seats. Once the Braves packed up and left Boston, a lot of fans felt they no longer had a team to be loyal to, and many found that they couldn't transfer their loyalty to Milwaukee. This same feeling would be felt four years later by Brooklyn fans when the Dodgers left for Los Angeles.

INTERLUDE ONE

From the time I was old enough to know what a baseball card was, I have never bothered to collect any modern players. Some people may say that this is just good business sense, but I know that I collect pre-1960 cards and memorabilia for a much bigger reason—my nostalgic appreciation. Baseball just seemed to be more fun then. I'm not saying that from 1960 to the present there haven't been any good ballplayers. I feel, however, that there haven't been any that could compare to our "old-time favorites" such as Joe DiMaggio, Babe Ruth, Warren Spahn, Duke Snider or any of the countless others who have made their mark in the record books.

As I was researching this book, a question arose that I had a hard time answering: "If the Braves had always had financial trouble stemming as far back as 1872, why didn't they leave Boston prior to 1952?" They had even been competing against the Red Sox since 1901 for patronage, so why didn't they leave Boston earlier? In order to answer this question correctly, I had to go back into the history of this country and see what year or years our country may have experienced any kind of sociological or economic boom. I also listened to what the former players I interviewed had to say. After all this questioning, it became apparent to me that the era in which these former tribesmen played passed us by too quickly. I'm sure it didn't happen all at once. It was a gradual change that occurred, and most of us probably didn't realize it until it was too late. For those of you who think that the United Sates started its moral decline in 1992 with the election of Bill Clinton to the presidency, I regret to inform you that you're wrong. It started when Ike left office—actually, it started in 1950 and roller coasted when Ike left office.

In 1950, we first saw the boom of the automobile. It became more affordable, and many homes came to the realization that they could afford to have two cars in their household. This helped to quicken the decline of public transportation as streetcars experienced a loss in patronage.

The first blow that came to Major League Baseball in the 1950s that changed the game forever for its players was the increased growth of air travel. This helped to accelerate the decline of the railroad passenger trains. This meant that the players could fly to St. Louis from Boston in a few hours, rather than traveling by train and taking two days for a one-way trip.

The proliferation of television viewing and a surge in radio audiences also had an impact on baseball. This gave the fans the opportunity to watch ballgames from the comfort of their own homes, meanwhile causing a disturbing decline in attendance at ballparks. This new entertainment medium caused America to become "preoccupied." Television shows such as *I Love Lucy*, Milton Berl's *Texaco Star Theatre* and Jackie Gleason and Sid Caesar's *Your Show of Shows* became distractions to the American public. All events (especially baseball) that relied upon gate receipts to survive started to suffer. The revenues from TV coverage, though minute by today's standards, helped offset the declining attendance to the parks, but unfortunately not enough to some of the ailing franchises like Boston. Television, which started out as a novelty, would wind up an institution by 1959.

The undisputed source for reliable baseball coverage in the 1950s was the *Sporting News*. This weekly newspaper was a familiar fixture on newsstands across the country. Some of the major events during the 1950s include: the Brinks Robbery (1950), the attempted assassination of President Truman (1950), the Kefauver Committee hearings (1951), the firing of General MacArthur (1951), the Korean Conflict (1950–1953) and the conquest of Everest (1953).

This was also the grand climax of the era of the concrete and steel ballparks. Each of these parks, although similar in design principle, brought its own unique personality to the game. The feeling and sense of neighborhood would soon be gone forever, as franchises moved and wrecking balls made way for modernization. The new parks are trying to resurrect the ambiance of the classical ballparks, but to no avail.

The events and developments of the 1950s had a direct and profound impact on American society, baseball and especially future generations. Even today, when a child takes the field, whether it be for a little league game or a high school game, I can't help but wonder if he's thinking about the game or how much money he'll make if he makes it to the big leagues. The 1950s were a golden era but one that changed the face of baseball forever and took our past from us.

It seems to me that, with each technological advancement our country makes, we can't help but lose our innocence and a part of our past. Baseball has remained that one constant throughout our country's history. It reminds us of our innocence. Television started out as a tool for our recreation and has turned into a way to follow our favorite baseball teams without going to the ballpark and enjoying the comradery of our fellow fans. We don't squawk when the owners increase the price of tickets to pay the overinflated salaries of the modern players with the overinflated egos. I understand that like everything else, baseball is a business, but somewhere along the way baseball has lost its blue-collar appeal. I guess an unknown sportswriter said it best when he wrote, "If there is sentiment in baseball, it comes exclusively through the turnstiles."

I have gone into the history of the early 1950s for one reason—this reason being that the Boston fans for years blamed Lou Perini for moving the team to Milwaukee, but we as a society each played a part in that move, whether it was driving to the park rather than taking the trolley or following the Braves on radio or television instead of going to the park.

Another contributing factor to the demise of Boston's National League franchise was the Red Sox. In the fifty-two years that the Braves competed against the Red Sox for patronage, only seven times did the Braves outdraw the Red Sox.

After I answered the first question, another one sprang to mind almost instantly. Where have these former players gone? Just like in the familiar song from Simon and Garfunkel titled "The Graduate" they ask, "Where have you gone, Joe DiMaggio?" I too asked the same.

Nearly everyone—even ballplayers—has led two lives at the very best. The first is the time of their glory, earned on the diamond and thrown back at them by the fans. The second is the long time after, when the years have taken them away from the lights, the crowds and the moments of physical genius and left them older and out of the game, for the most part in obscurity.

What happened next? This is the eternal question, and this is where our story continues. In the days after the Braves had found their way west and the old Boston team had disbanded and withered away into retirement, I went looking for these heroes of yesteryear to ask, "What comes after the brief public lives of such star athletes?"

I could never understand why my father's face lit up as he recalled ball games and players from his youth. However, after I had met these men, I realized that meeting them was not something to either dismiss or let anyone else dismiss in arrogant ignorance. It had become part of me; it was something to be proud of. Even though it may be thirty or so years too late, I have finally realized why my father would seem like he was in a kind of daydream when he spoke of the Braves. It is because one judges age by one's contemporaries. If they were old, then he himself was old, but if he viewed them young and vibrant then he would view himself the same way.

In the chapters ahead, we will travel back with former Braves players and fans. We will hear their thoughts and memories of the Braves and Braves Field and what it meant to them. We will see what happened to our former icons after they left Boston, when they retired from baseball and what they think of the game today.

CHAPTER 8
A VISIT TO BRAVES FIELD TODAY

While in the midst of researching the history of the Braves, I was put in touch with a man by the name of George Altison who then put me in touch with Bob Brady. These two men play an instrumental role in the Boston Braves Historical Association. The association has one objective: to preserve the memory of Boston's only National League franchise. When I contacted these men, I was hoping for any light that they might be able to shed on the history of the Braves. Instead I found my proverbial light at the end of the tunnel. They informed me that on October 6, 1996, they would be sponsoring a Braves player/fan reunion. At this event, former players would be present to tell stories and reminisce, not only with each other, but with the fans who would be present as well. Before I realized what I was about to undertake, I was making arrangements to head to Boston.

October 6 was a Sunday, and the reunion was scheduled to start at 10:00 a.m. The traffic was light as I made my way into the city. It was as if the city knew that these former warriors of the diamond were back in town, and this was its way of paying homage to them. As I drove down Commonwealth Avenue through Kenmore Square and past the historic Citgo sign that has become a landmark of Red Sox baseball in Boston, I felt impelled toward old familiar places. Traveling down Commonwealth Avenue, it's hard not to notice the public transit trolleys that run up and down the street with iron wheels keening. These trolleys are similar to the ones that used to take fans and ballplayers to Braves Field. They now transport Boston University college students to and from downtown Boston. Both sides of Commonwealth Avenue,

Sibby Sisti attempting a bunt in the 1948 World Series. *Courtesy of BPL.*

from Kenmore Square to the Allston city limits, are predominantly owned by
Boston University, including what remains of Braves Field.

I was lucky enough to find a parking space almost in front of the building
in which the reunion was to take place. After I parked the car and got out, I
noticed that I had about forty-five minutes before they would open the doors

A Visit to Braves Field Today

View of the Jury Box. This was Holmes Country. *Courtesy of BPL.*

to the college auditorium in which this event was to be held. As I looked around for a coffee shop, I noticed that there was a McDonalds about a block and a half down the street, so I started for it. The closer I was getting to McDonalds, the more things looked familiar to me. I noticed a street sign that read Harry Agganis Drive. Just as I was about to cross this street and enter McDonalds, I realized why it was vaguely familiar to me. Years earlier it was called Gaffney Street. This was the street that trolleys would turn off of Commonwealth Avenue to take patrons to Braves Field's main entrance.

Memories of every Braves story my father told me came flooding into consciousness. As I walked behind the former main entrance and headed toward the right field pavilion, I couldn't help but feel privileged—privileged to be walking on the same hallowed ground that my forefathers had walked only years earlier. As I headed into the only remaining pavilion, I became surrounded by memories so thick that I had to brush them away from my face.

It seemed almost psychotic to me, but as I stood inside the old pavilion, I could've sworn that I heard the rustling of long-ago crowds and the hum of a loudspeaker as Jim Britt's voice bellowed throughout the park. This dream continued for me until I walked out of one of the pavilion portals into the daylight. I stood outside of the portal and looked to my left, where a tall stand of faceless brick buildings had replaced the old grandstand seating. Even though the Braves had abandoned the field many years earlier, I had an eerie feeling that I was in the presence of ghosts from seasons past. No matter how eerie the feeling was, I felt a strange peace surround my soul. I could only compare the peace I felt to the conversion of St. Paul being thrown from the saddle of his horse to the roadside where, for several verses, he sat basking in Christianity. As I turned around and headed back toward the auditorium, I thought, "Is that the mind's last, soundless, dying cry, who will remember?" There were no cheering crowds as my wrenching but joyous voyage ended in the question: "Who will remember?" Then it occurred to me, just as it occurred to Hamlet when Horatio wanted to fall on his sword when Hamlet was dying. Hamlet told him not to kill himself, because Hamlet himself was dying and if Horatio died, then there would be no one to tell Hamlet's story. You see a dead man has a skull, and a skull has no tongue; but a live man has a tongue, and it is only through a tongue that a story goes on. Therefore, I feel that I am not only compelled but somehow chosen to be that tongue.

As I entered the auditorium and paid the ten-dollar admission, I looked around for these former heroes of my father's youth. The foyer of the auditorium was filled mostly with men whose ages ranged anywhere from late fifties to mid-seventies. The historical association had some tables set up in the lobby with displays of Braves memorabilia. Around 10:30 a.m., the announcement was made for everyone to head downstairs to the auditorium. The auditorium seated approximately three hundred people, and there were about another twenty people standing in the back, including several of the news reporters from the local area.

For the next hour and a half the audience was held captive by the stories of these former players. After the formality of the event was over, I was given what I consider the chance of a lifetime: to interview these former titans of the diamond.

I looked around the hallways of the auditorium, and it occurred to me that no matter how old ballplayers get, the art of bench jockeying returns when they are among old teammates.

I stood in the hallway and watched in relative solitude as Sibby Sisti was being interviewed by a reporter from the New England Sports Network.

"Spahn and Sain and pray for rain." This was the cry of the fans during the 1948 season.
Courtesy of NBHOF.

Then I heard Johnny Logan holler down the hall, "Hey Sibby, you telling more lies?" It was at this point that I spotted a man surrounded by reporters. He had a special glint in his eye as he recalled his 1945 hitting streak. As he stood there, it occurred to me that this man was Tommy Holmes. As much as Boston fans and sportswriters adorn Tommy with their praise and admiration, he seems to feel that they are the ones who deserve his gratitude for remembering him after all these years. In his eyes he is just a ballplayer who did his best. Tommy was accompanied by his wife, Lillian. I immediately sensed the pride she had in her husband's many years in professional baseball, as she proudly displayed several trinkets of Tommy's career in the Major Leagues—sort of like her own personal Hall of Fame necklace. She also had a picture of her hero pinned on the front of her sweater. Such devotion is indeed rare and seldom seen!

The Braves batboys. *Courtesy of George Altison.*

The 1948 Braves celebrating Gardner, Massachusetts Day. Billy Southworth, Earl Torgeson, Bob Elliott and Tommy Holmes take time for a picture and blow off a little steam before a game. *Courtesy of George Altison.*

A Visit to Braves Field Today

Tommy Holmes has this friendly charm and constant grin that make you feel like you've known him your entire life. A nicer man you'll never meet!

He was born Thomas Francis Holmes on March 29, 1918, in Brooklyn, New York. He broke into professional baseball in 1937. The Braves acquired him in 1941 from the New York Yankees. George Weis told Tommy that Casey Stengel wanted him and that if Casey couldn't make a Major League player out of him then no one could.

Tommy played in right field from 1942 to 1951 and had what no player in Major League history has had before or since: the Jury Box! He was adored by Boston fans, who held a fierce loyalty to him. On one occasion, Holmes was hit on the wrist by a pitch from Alpha Brazzle and had to leave the game. Nanny Fernandez quietly walked out to the outfield and hollered to the Jury Box that Holmes was hurt and couldn't play. The fans booed Fernandez anyway! When Holmes would return to the outfield after being up at bat, the fans would cheer no matter if he struck out or hit a homer. Holmes would always return the gesture by either waving broadly or clasping his hands over his head like a prizefighter.

It was still hard to buy a car at the war's end, but that didn't stop the Braves fans. They simply all chipped in and bought him one!

A generous gesture such as this is evidence of the fans' undying loyalty to Tommy. Holmes was the fans' baby, and they wouldn't tolerate anybody else in right field. The Red Sox had the "splendid splinter" Ted Williams, but the Braves had the "sweet swing" of Tommy Holmes.

One of the Braves' biggest fans was Lolly Hopkins. She would sit in the stands with her megaphone and pass out candy to the Braves team and tootsie rolls to the visiting team. One day before a game, Tommy and his teammates wanted to show their appreciation to Lolly for her patronage, so they presented her with a bracelet. This was just another way the Braves club treated their fans like family.

When Billy Southworth experimented with Holmes in left field and Johnny Barrett in right, the Jury Box fans rioted! The next day, Tommy was back.

Mike McCormick received the same treatment the next season, when Southworth briefly platooned him with Tommy. Tommy fondly remembers hitting safely in his thirty-fourth game of the 1945 season. The game was against Brooklyn, and Preacher Roe was on the mound. The first pitch was low and away, but the second pitch Tommy hit. The next day he questioned Preacher Roe about the first pitch, and Roe responded, "You ain't gonna hit my first pitch, Tommy." Tommy replied, "No, but I hit the second one." When I questioned Tommy about Preacher Roe's infamous spitball, his reply was, "You just had to pray." Tommy said that the pitcher he feared

Tommy Holmes receiving a brand-new car from the fans at Braves Field. *Courtesy of author's collection.*

the most when he came to the plate was Ewell "The Whip" Blackwell. He was a menacing six feet, six inches but painfully thin. The sidearmer threw a vicious ninety-five-mile-per-hour sinking ball. When I asked Tommy what he thought was the most important aspect of hitting, he said it was "the eyes," and that is why, in his opinion, Wade Boggs is the best hitter in baseball today.

At five feet, ten inches and 180 pounds, Tommy didn't seem like your average .300 hitter, but as we know, things aren't always as they seem. Tommy was a consistent .300 hitter. As a Brave outfielder, he hit .309 in 1944, .352 in 1945, .310 in 1946, .309 in 1947, .325 in 1948 and .298 in 1950. Tommy also informed me that Sibby Sisti was the greatest relay man he ever had. In the middle of the 1951 season, Tommy was chosen to replace Billy Southworth as manager. On May 31, 1952, he was succeeded by Charley Grimm. From 1952 to 1957, Tommy was with the Brooklyn Dodgers organization.

For the next couple of years, Tommy worked with kids in sandlot baseball. He joined the Mets in 1963 and is now the director of the Amateur Baseball Foundation for New York Mets.

Raising of the 1948 pennant at Braves Field. *Courtesy of author's collection.*

It truly amazes me how selfless and giving Tommy is. Since his departure from professional baseball, he has devoted his time to helping kids advance their baseball careers. After my interview with Tommy, I realized that while most ballplayers rate their careers on personal stats, Tommy rates his by the loyalty of the Jury Box and the number of people he was able to help.

An interesting aspect of this reunion was that the historical association did not pay these former players, nor did it pay the players for their travel and hotel expenses. The players were invited to attend and came of their own accord. Most of them stayed with friends on the Cape and enjoyed a couple of rounds of golf the day before the reunion. The association not only invited the players but also the batboys.

As I watched and spoke with these men, I realized that a special quality of the old Boston team was a concern and compassion for others less famous and less fortunate than themselves.

The Braves management always tried to treat the patrons as family. This feeling of family can still be felt today, as I spoke to two former batboys for the team.

The first batboy I spoke to was Charles Chronopoulos, a batboy for the Braves from 1939 to 1950. Charles said he got the job one day when he was hanging around outside after the game. The clubhouse guy, who was called Shorty, came out and asked Charles if he wanted to make a buck fifty. The inquisitive nine-year-old agreed and asked what he had to do. Shorty told him to empty the barrels, shine the shoes and clean the spikes. Shorty, being impressed with the kid's enthusiasm, asked him to return the next day. Charles did, and he was given the job of batboy. He said the players who started out as his idols became his friends. People like Tommy Holmes would make sure that he went to church every week; the rest of the players would look out for him too. Charles told me that he wished that every kid were given the opportunity that he was given. It also saddens him to hear that some of the players have passed on. "They are very special people," he said. "Somewhere, along the way, they touched you with a story or a joke. It's just sad because we were such a close unit."

Frank McNulty, who was the Braves batboy for the visiting teams, told me he started with the Braves in 1945 when he was fifteen years old. When asked about his years with the Braves he said, "Much to my wife's chagrin, I would have to say, that the best years of my life were from fifteen to eighteen."

As I interviewed these former players and batboys I realized that, as fans, we don't truly appreciate the most significant times in our lives until they have passed us by. As I entertained this thought, I decided that there was no better way to give you a looking glass view into the thoughts and feelings of an avid fan than to interview one.

I was lucky enough in my quest to meet and interview one of the most enthusiastic Braves fans ever, John Delmore. John has been a Braves fan since his earliest memories of baseball. He still remembers the 1948 season fondly:

I was at the game in September of 1948 when the Braves beat the Giants on a Bob Elliott home run and went on to play Cleveland in the World Series. I still remember racing home from school, jumping fences and everything, just to catch the latter part of the ballgame. It was the ninth inning. The Braves were ahead 1–0 and Johnny Sain finally got the last out—a fly ball to center field. I ran out of the house to rub it in to all my American League friends that the Braves had won! I was a young kid when I came out by streetcar the night before and got a ticket to game six of the World Series. I sat in the Jury Box and watched my beloved Braves lose game six of the World Series, but I was still proud of them. A few years later, as a young lad of fifteen, the first job I ever had was a concessioner at Braves Field. I would sell scorecards and peanuts in the right field pavilion. We'd get out to the ballpark early and set up our venue. We'd always be there around morning batting practice, and the Braves players, especially Tommy Holmes (who is the nicest guy that ever came down the pike), would shoot the bull with us. He would even toss us a ball if nobody was looking because they were tightwads back then. They didn't throw balls around like they do now. Those were great days. The Braves were a blue-collar team, unlike the Red Sox, who were Yawkey's millionaires. The Braves were a lunch pail brigade, and we never expected a lot from them. We felt worse for them than we did for ourselves when they lost. That was the kind of love we had for the ball club. I was in the navy, in boot camp, in Maryland. I was so heartbroken, I didn't know whether to go AWOL or take emergency leave, or do something, to come home and convince Perini not to move the team. But that's one of the early lessons in life, I guess. That you don't always get things the way you want. But it was a sad day in my life when they left. I've never had any regrets for following the Braves. If anything, they've given me a lot of fond memories!

CHAPTER 9
BRAVES PLAYER/FAN REUNION

While wandering among old Braves, I realized that they looked neither better nor worse than the pictures I remembered. Mortality seems to embrace aging ballplayers. Our heroes of yesteryear seem to live in continual twilight. They retire in reality but are eternal in our memory. Only the fan grows old with each passing season—the player remains youthful. Babe Ruth once said, "A man who has put away his baseball togs, after an eventful life in the game, must live on his memories…some good…some bad."

Most players were farmers who just hoped that, at the end of a Major League career, they would be able to buy more farmland or replace two mules with a tractor. The majority of the ballplayers from the city usually bought hardware stores.

These former players are just simple blue-collar guys. They don't regard themselves as gods. They don't believe the world owes them something. If anything, they feel they owe the world something because they were more fortunate than most and were able to play big league ball. Some of the other players present at the reunion included Sibby Sisti, Johnny Logan, Dick Donovan, Gene Conley and Art Johnson. I interviewed Sibby Sisti in the hallway, just outside the auditorium. Throughout the whole interview, Sibby kept stressing to me that "it wasn't just Spahn and Sain. There were twenty-five other guys who were put together, and came together, as a team." When I asked Sibby what was special about the 1948 Braves team, he told me, "Whether it was a base hit, or a home run, or some kind of a fielding feat, whatever the case was, you don't win pennants with one or two guys, you win 'em with twenty-five guys." What stood out in his mind was a relief pitcher by the name of Nelson Potter. Sibby commented on by saying, "He did a tremendous job for us. He came in during the eighth and ninth innings to hold a one-run lead. I don't think he ever got the credit I thought he deserved." As I spoke further with Sibby, he told me about several notable moments that came to mind. The first was when he first came to the club and manager Billy Southworth came into the dugout. Southworth would change his catchers depending on who was pitching and hitting and who was in the outfield. When Southworth came into the dugout, he looked at Sibby and said, "In case I need anybody, you're my next catcher." Sibby said when he heard that he almost fell off his seat. He said, "From then on, if I wasn't playing I was in the bullpen, helping to warm up the pitchers. But with all my years with the Braves, I played seven positions but never catcher. If I did, I would be able to say that I played eight positions instead of seven."

I think Sibby's most memorable season was 1948. He told me that he beat Alvin Dark out for the shortstop position and that, in the middle of the season, Eddy Stanky broke his ankle. He further added, "And it just so happened that I played in one ballgame, that changed my whole career, for that season. The game was against the Cardinals and the bases were loaded. Southworth was going to send in a pinch hitter, but there was just Johnny Sain and myself who could pinch hit because Southworth had used everybody else in the game. I looked at Johnny and said, 'You better grab a bat.' The Cardinals got two runs in the top of the eleventh inning. In the bottom of the eleventh, we had the bases loaded with two out when I got up to hit. I hit the ball between Stan Musial and Enos Slaughter to win the game. It was a big game because we were fighting for the pennant. After that, I got in to play regularly."

Sibby's fondest memories are those of the fans. He says, "Even though, from 1939 to 1942, they didn't draw very well because it was always a Red Sox town, we were well liked. It's always nice to have people remember you and think about you. I know I feel great when I get a request for an autograph, even if it's from some young lad."

After my interview with Sibby, I noticed a rather stocky man speaking with fans in the hallway. This jovial guy was Johnny Logan. I walked up to him and requested an interview. Needless to say, I was born too late to see him play. He had this look about him that just said, "Give me a chance." In my opinion, if there ever was a person who was born a ballplayer, it was Johnny Logan. If you look at other former ballplayers you can almost picture them selling insurance or driving a truck, but not

Bob Elliott crossing home plate after hitting his second home run in game five. *Courtesy of NBHOF.*

Johnny—he looks like a ballplayer even today. I asked Johnny how he came to Boston, and he told me, "Well, I remember I spent three years with the Milwaukee Brewers in Triple-A and my next move was the big leagues. I really groomed myself those three years so I could come up to Boston, but the Braves had a great shortstop by the name of Alvin Dark. Once they made the move to Milwaukee, that meant to me that there might be a possibility that I might get a chance to start. And when I got the chance, I was determined that I was going to succeed, somehow.

Luckily with guys like Sibby Sisti, Bob Elliott and Tommy Holmes, they really helped groom me into a Boston Braves baseball player."

I guess this special grooming that Johnny received, along with his hard work and determination, was the reason that he became one of the spark plugs of the Braves' contending teams of the mid-1950s. Johnny became the Braves' regular shortstop in 1952, hitting a solid .283 in 117 games. For the next five seasons his average never dipped below .273. Johnny's best year was 1955, when he hit .297 with 13 homers, 95 runs and 83 RBIs. His lifetime average is .268. When I asked his feelings about the club's move to Milwaukee, Johnny said, "I didn't know exactly what was going to happen in Milwaukee, but I was going back home. We hit new territory by making the move."

When I asked Johnny how he felt about being back in Boston for the player/fan reunion, his response was filled with sentiment: "Coming back to Boston reminds me of my first base hit, my first home run and my first Major League game in Braves Field, and it's a thrill!"

The player/fan reunion was quickly drawing to an end, but I still wanted to interview three more former players. I was able to catch Dick Donovan and Gene Conley before they left. I asked Dick Donovan, who pitched for the Braves, what he thought was the reason this team had such an appeal to the fans. He replied, "We were the underdogs, constantly struggling. The Red Sox had great ballplayers like Ted Williams, but more people could identify with us, and this helped raise a lot of loyalty." When asked how he wanted the Braves to be remembered, his answer couldn't help but bring a smile to my face. "Favorably," he said, "they did their best."

Gene Conley, who is no stranger to Boston, having pitched with the Braves and played for the Celtics at the same time, had kind of a boyish grin on his face as he told me about the first time he pitched in Braves Field. "I was brought up in 1952 and only pitched one game in Boston. I was twenty-one years old and lasted five innings against the Dodgers. That was my career in Braves Field. But just to be a teammate with these former Braves players is really quite a thrill." When asked about being a two-sport athlete, his reply was direct and honest: "At the time I didn't think it was too difficult, but when I think back now I did miss a lot of spring training. Because I was with the Celtics, and after the playoff, when we'd finish, unfortunately, baseball season had already started. And I'd miss eight or ten games, and I wouldn't get in much training, as far as pitching. I would go down and work out with a high school team or a minor league team for a couple of weeks. It really wasn't good for my arm. I did that for thirteen seasons."

Aerial view of Braves Field with lights. *Courtesy of author's collection.*

I almost missed Art Johnson as he was heading out the door of the lobby. He was attempting to leave in time to meet with several former players at a local restaurant, but he was gracious enough to agree to an interview.

Art Johnson pitched for the Braves from 1940 to 1943 and still fondly remembers his first game with the team. "In my first game as a Brave, Casey sent me out to the bullpen. About the fourth inning a line drive hits Lefty Joe Sullivan—I thought it hit him on the knee. So he calls a time out, and Casey runs out to the mound. They were holding a conference on the mound, and all of a sudden, Casey starts waving to the bullpen. I came running out to the mound, and I'm thinking, 'Wow, my first Major League game.' So I say, 'Mr. Stengel, I'll do my best to get you out of this inning.' Casey then says, 'Hell, kid, I don't want you to pitch. Lefty Joe Sullivan broke the web in his glove with that line drive, and he wants to use your glove.' That was my initiation into the Boston Braves...Someone asked me what was the most wonderful thing that happened to me when I was with the Braves, and I responded, 'Seeing the loyal fans come out to Braves Field every day.'"

As the reunion disbanded, I headed for my car and got in. I turned around on a side street and headed back down Commonwealth Avenue. Just as I approached a red light at Kenmore Square and came to a stop, I glanced at the car next to me. In it were Johnny Logan, Sibby Sisti and Billy Sullivan. I watched them as they pointed to different buildings in the area. If I had only one wish at that moment, it would have been to be able to see Boston through their eyes!

CHAPTER 10
SAM GENTILE

Now that the reunion was over, I headed for Everett, Massachusetts. The day before, I had scheduled an interview with Sam Gentile, who lives in Everett.

Everett is approximately fifteen minutes from Boston. It is a good-size city, with a lot of industry and three-decker homes. Most of the people who grew up there remain there to raise their children, so there is a sense of small-town pride within this city.

Sam lives on Central Avenue. This street is located on a mild hill off of Ferry Street, a main road, and is lined with modest homes. The families on this street are predominantly Italian and Irish in ancestry. Mr. Gentile's home is modest and neat in appearance. It is a two-story home with an enclosed porch. I arrived at Sam's house and knocked on the front door. Sam greeted me at the door and invited me in. He walked me through his home and into the kitchen, where he had a roast in the oven.

Sammy seemed to be surprised that I wanted to interview him. He felt that his brief, three-month career with the Braves was of little or no significance to the team. He offered me a beer, and we sat down at his kitchen table.

From 1941 to 1945, the Braves brought up a lot of new talent from the minors to replace the talent that Uncle Sam drafted for the war effort. Here I sat with one of those young men, a local boy from Everett, Sam Gentile.

Sam graduated from Everett High School, all scholastic and captain of the football, basketball and baseball teams. He was signed by the Red Sox and sent off to the minors. As he moved up through the minors, his last stop was Danville, Virginia, where he led the league in hitting, at .389. He played with players like Pesky, Parnell and Tex Hughson. When spring training rolled around, he was expecting to go but instead was told to report to Louisville. Sammy's reply?

"I won't go to Louisville," I told them. I also told them that I thought I had done well enough to at least go to spring training. They told me that they had enough left-handed hitters from Ted Williams on down. I could see that now, but back then I just wanted to at least go to spring training. I balked and they balked, and I remained in Everett. Finally, I got my outright release from them because I felt I wasn't being treated fairly. There was no spring training that year because of the war. The Braves held training that year at the Armory in Boston. Casey Stengel was the manager, and he liked the way I ran, so the Braves signed me for $6,500 a year. Casey made me the starting center fielder against the Red Sox in the City Series. I got two hits in the first game against the Red Sox, and from then on I was the starting center fielder for the Braves. In my first game at Braves Field I had two hits against the Giants, the first hit being a long double over Mel Ott's head. It bounced off the right field wall, which was about 420 feet. We lost the game 2–1, but I scored the only run. The next night, Casey was struck by a car in Kenmore Square, and the manager that replaced him didn't see eye to eye with me. I got in, now and then, to pinch hit or whatever. Shortly after, I was drafted into the navy (which ate up about four years of playing time). When I came back from the war, I wasn't in shape to return to the Braves, although I could've returned to play ball under the GI Bill of Rights. So I took a manager/player position with the Braves' minor league team in Pawtucket. From there I was sent to Nashua, New Hampshire, where I managed one of the greatest pitching batteries in the history of baseball: Don Newcombe and Roy Campanella.

The Braves later sold these two future Hall of Famers to the Brooklyn franchise. From there, Sammy took a job as the director of recreation in Everett because he wanted to be closer to his family. He also helped establish a Little League and some Pony Leagues. I asked Sammy what it was like to be managed by Casey Stengel, and this is what he had to say: "Casey was one of the best managers there ever was. He was a very psychic person. He would sit in the dugout, and something seemed to tell him which pinch hitter to use at the right time. He was a wonder; you'd have to love him on the bench."

Sammy's comments on ballplayers (then compared to now) couldn't help but bring a smile to my face.

It was harder to get to the Majors in my day. There weren't that many leagues. Farm teams were tougher then. You were buckin' fifteen outfielders to get a job. In my day, they had six farm teams. Now they probably have around fifteen. In my day you had to produce or you didn't have a job. You couldn't hit .220 or .240 like they do today. You had to hit .350 as an infielder and .390 as an outfielder or you lose your job. This was just the make of baseball. The game today has too many prima donnas. In my day they were gentlemen, autographing and everything. You never heard of taking money for an autograph. And all these special agents that are getting rich off the ballplayers, I don't go for that. I could never turn down a kid who was in the stands, wanting an autograph, without busting my fanny to give it to him. In my day, you loved the game—you didn't even think about the money, because the average person only made $70 or $80 a week. Wally Berger was the best outfielder besides Tommy Holmes. He was also one of the best power hitters I know of. He treated us rookies fairly, but we had to keep our place with him. You couldn't say anything, especially when you were looking for a guy's job. When I played, the ball was more deadly than it is today and the uniforms were heavier. We only had two uniforms—one for home and one for on the road. I advise the youth today to take up catching. When I speak at a Little League banquet I generally ask who the third string catcher is on a certain club. Ninety-five percent of the time nobody can answer me. Then they'll give me the first string catcher's name, so I'll ask them who the second string catcher is and they still can't answer me. Then I'll say, "You just threw away a $70,000 a year job for just sitting on the bench."

I asked him to compare the differences between the Braves and the Red Sox—here's what Sammy had to say.

"The Red Sox had Tom Yawkey, a great man, but a one-way ball club. The Braves weren't a high-paying ball club, but they treated you fairly. The Braves were more colorful and they played a closer game of baseball, with more bunting—they played for runs. The Red Sox wanted the long ball, and a lot of times they'd get it. But the National League was more adept at base stealing than the American League."

As the interview ended, I thanked Sam for his time and headed for my car. I started to drive off, and then a thought occurred to me. Maybe Sam's baseball career didn't amount to much, but his minor league coaching sure did, as well as what he was able to do for the community.

I only wish that more people would follow Mr. Gentile's example of putting family and community first. Then maybe we wouldn't have a nation of lost children. In my eyes, Sam is the last of a dying breed of real gentlemen!

INTERLUDE TWO

Throughout this book we have tracked the history of the Boston Braves, a club that started out as one of many loosely managed confederation teams and wound up a vast and organized entity. This team and our country have grown up together. They both experienced a golden age and a crash, simultaneously. As I traced the history of this team I couldn't help but notice the parallel between what was happening in the great pastime and America itself. Both the game and the country were enormously affected by the media and mass communication. We also saw the rise of a naïve game, its early refinement and the emerging sophistication of players and fans. This club was more real, more romantic than most. The Boston Braves had a sweetness about them, a sort of clumsy beauty that reminds us of our youth. Even though it has been over sixty years since the Braves called Boston home, this team still has a power to intrigue that far outweighs portraits or words. One of the biggest factors of the Braves' success was the fact that they never quit or gave up.

After meeting these former Braves, I quickly realized that, although it was their baseball skills that drew me to them, it was the content of their character that made them special.

View of Braves Field from the grandstand. *Courtesy of NBHOF.*

It has been said that from simple times come extraordinary people. As I pondered this thought, I questioned what was has changed since these men were born.

Well, to start, they were born before: television, penicillin, polio shots, frozen foods, plastic, contact lenses, "the pill," radar, credit cards, split atoms, ballpoint pens, gay rights, computers, the Internet, therapy, house husbands, air conditioning, dishwashers, man walking on the moon and guys wearing earrings.

In their era, a chip meant a piece of wood and software wasn't even a word. "Made in Japan" meant junk, and pizza, McDonalds and instant coffee were unheard of. For a nickel they could ride a streetcar, make a phone call, buy a Coke or buy enough stamps to mail one letter and two postcards.

Cigarette smoking was fashionable, grass was mowed and Coke was a cold drink. They could buy a new Chevy for $600, but who could afford it? They made do with what they had and still believed in the sanctity of marriage. Their generation gave the world most of the good things we enjoy today.

When I was growing up, anytime I complained about something my father would say, "That's because you didn't live through the Depression." My father is also from this older generation, the age of eighty now his unwelcome beckoner. I am grateful for the pleasures I have been able to derive from this generation's hard work and perseverance.

Every father dreams of the blissful time to come when he can take his son or daughter to their first baseball game. The dream begins when a man first learns that he is going to be a father. His thoughts immediately drift to the first game of catch they will have in the backyard. After this thought, he runs to the local sports store to buy the future child a baseball glove—this is where the legacy of baseball begins.

My father lived and died with the Boston Braves. He lived a little in 1948, and he died a lot when they moved to Milwaukee. As it has been for so many fathers and sons, baseball is a way of sharing experiences between my father and me. It was not the only way, but at times it proved to be one of the easiest. On a few occasions, we went to see the Red Sox play. Most frequent were the anecdotes or bits and pieces about players he had seen or particular plays that became fixed in his memory. Those moments become dearer to me with each passing year. That is because I now realize that my father was sharing something with me. He was taking me into his confidence.

Going to my first game was one of the last times I would ever find myself looking at a picture in which every single detail was new to me. In later years I would come to miss this sheer novelty. Nothing in life can replace the enriching experience of attending a game. From the 1920s until the mid-1960s,

Above: Sliding home at Braves Field. *Courtesy of author's collection.*

Left: Fan favorite Tommy Holmes and Johnny Sain celebrating a win during the 1948 World Series. *Courtesy of author's collection.*

baseball was the dominant sport in America. Besides being a symbol of our country, it is also our security blanket. Fathers and their children are the keepers of the baseball flame. Astro turf, free agency, contentious umpires and overpaid players did not exist during the Braves' years in Boston. I guess I am just a stuffy old traditionalist in some people's eyes. I abhor change in my own life, and I don't accept alterations in my favorite sport too well, either. Don't get me wrong—I still love baseball even though I don't entirely understand it anymore. I long for the days when the dominance of the game had an impact on every American. What has happened to the game of my youth and the game of my father's youth?

How I long for the days when baseball was considered the ultimate portrait of elegance. Baseball has always given the American boy a hero. My father's hero was Alvin Dark; even today he still looks up to him.

Baseball is forever summer—cut grass, chalk and the first awkward feel of a glove that's much too big. Always we are touched by baseball's unfailing innocence and its ability to conjure up the long golden days of a simpler time. Baseball is our childhood. This was a moment of pure baseball at a time before money, lawsuits, steroids and business interests made it less of a game. What keeps pulling us back to the game? Is it our belief that legends can still happen right there on the diamond—that men can be heroes at least for a play? Somewhere out there is an endless and wonderful summer at Braves Field waiting for us all.

CHAPTER 11

LIFE AFTER BASEBALL

The following is a partial list of former Boston Braves players and what they did after they no longer were players.

Tommy Holmes managed in the Dodgers and Braves farm systems from 1953 to 1957. When actor Anthony Perkins starred in the 1957 movie *Fear Strikes Out* about centerfielder Jimmy Piersall, Tommy instructed Perkins how to look like a ballplayer. Unfortunately, Perkins didn't have any athletic ability and did not look natural in the portrayal. In 1973, Holmes became director of amateur baseball relations for the New York Mets, a post he held for three decades until he retired at eighty-six. He passed away of natural causes at the age of ninety-one in an assisted living facility in Florida on April 14, 2008.

Sibby Sisti coached and managed in the minors for many years after his baseball career. In 1984, he had a bit part in the film *The Natural* starring Robert Redford. Sisti portrayed the Pittsburgh manager. He was also a consultant on the film, helping to ensure the movie had a 1930s feel to it. For many years, Sibby would attend the player/fan reunions and announce his latest royalty check from the movie, an amount that never ventured above five dollars. Sibby also said that if they ever make a sequel to the movie, he would tell the pitcher to throw at Redford. These comments would usually bring uproarious laughter from the crowd. Sibby passed away at age eighty-five in Amherst, New York, on April 24, 2006.

Earl Torgeson retired from baseball in 1961. He was married twice and was often seen sitting quietly in the stands of his children's sporting events.

In retirement, he worked as a stockbroker for a brief time. He later owned and operated Camp Forsyte, a sports camp for underprivileged children. In 1965, he and his second wife moved to Everett, Washington, where he grew up. His next job was director of parks for Snohomish County. He also briefly managed the Newark Co-Pilots and then the Clinton Pilots, succeeding Sibby Sisti. In 1972, he was elected county commissioner and served a four-year term. While in office, he was charged and tried for allegedly misappropriating funds and county material and labor. He successfully defended himself and was acquitted of all charges. He later worked for a timber company and served as county director of emergency management. He passed away on November 8, 1990, of leukemia.

After his retirement, Warren Spahn managed the Tulsa Oilers for five seasons from 1967 to 1971. He also coached for the Mexico City Tigers. He was a pitching coach with the Cleveland Indians and later a minor league team for the California Angels. He also went to Japan for six years and coached for the Hiroshima Toyo Carp. Spahn passed away at his home in Broken Arrow, Oklahoma, from natural causes on November 24, 2003.

Johnny Sain finished his career with the Kansas City Athletics in 1956. He worked as a pitching coach for the Yankees, Twins, Tigers, White Sox and Braves. He passed away at age eighty-nine at his home in Downers Grove, Illinois.

Phil Masi passed away at age seventy-four on March 29, 1990. Upon his death, his will revealed that he was really out on the famous pick-off play in the 1948 World Series.

Eddie Stanky managed the Cardinals and White Sox. In 1969, he became the head baseball coach of the University of South Alabama. He returned to Major League Baseball in 1977 and managed the Texas Rangers for one game. He immediately resigned and returned to his former post at South Alabama. He passed away at age eighty-two.

Alvin Dark worked as a manager for the San Francisco Giants, Kansas City Athletics, Cleveland Indians, Oakland Athletics and the San Diego Padres. At ninety years old, he is the oldest living manager of a World Series–winning, pennant-winning or postseason team. He currently resides with his wife in Easley, South Carolina.

Sam Gentile worked many years for the City of Everett, Massachusetts. When he passed away on May 4, 1998, his adopted city named the recreation center in his honor.

Gene Conley founded a paper company after retiring from professional sports. He worked at the paper company for thirty-six years before retiring. He and his wife currently reside in Waterville Valley, New Hampshire.

Johnny Logan played for the Nankai Hawks in Japan in 1964 after his Major League career. He currently resides in Milwaukee, Wisconsin.

Del Crandall managed the Milwaukee Brewers and the Seattle Mariners. He also managed in the minor leagues for the Los Angeles Dodgers. He later worked as a sports announcer for the Chicago White Sox from 1985 to 1988 and the Brewers from 1992 to 1994. He currently resides in Brea, California.

Eddie Matthews has the distinction of being the only Brave to play for Boston, Milwaukee and Atlanta. He managed the Braves from 1972 to 1974 and was elected to the Baseball Hall of Fame in 1978. He passed away in 2001 from complications of pneumonia in La Jolla, California.

Eddie Joost moved to Hawaii after he retired from baseball. He worked for Wilson Sporting Goods for many years. He was a very active supporter of the Philadelphia Athletics Historical Society Museum. He passed away at the age of ninety-four at his home in Fair Oaks, California, in 2011.

Bob Elliott managed several minor league teams after his baseball career. He did manage in the Kansas City Athletics and the Los Angeles Angels systems. Elliott died at age forty-nine in San Diego after suffering a ruptured vein in his windpipe on May 4, 1966.

Connie Ryan was a coach and minor league manager for Atlanta during the 1970s. In 1977, he began the season as a coach for the Texas Rangers and took over as manager for six games. He passed away on January 3, 1996, at age seventy-five at his home in Louisiana.

Bill Voiselle continued to pitch for minor league clubs after his last appearance as a Major League player. He passed away at home just two days after his eighty-sixth birthday.

Vern Bickford worked as an auto dealer, traveling salesman and a carpenter after baseball. He passed away on May 6, 1960, from cancer at the age of thirty-nine.

Nelson Potter returned to Mount Morris, where he owned and operated the Town and Country Lanes for fifteen years. He sold the business and, for the next thirteen years, worked as the Mount Morris Township supervisor. He passed away in 1990 at the age of seventy-nine.

Roy Hartsfield had a successful career after baseball as a manager in the minor leagues. From 1977 to 1979, he managed the expansion team the Toronto Blue Jays. He passed away from complications of liver cancer on January 15, 2011, at the age of eighty-five.

Norm Roy was a standout athlete at Waltham High School in Waltham, Massachusetts, before signing with the Braves. He passed away on March 22, 2011, in Nashua, New Hampshire.

Johnny Antonelli returned to Rochester, New York, after retiring from baseball. He ran a very successful chain of Firestone tire stores bearing his name. He is now fully retired and enjoys spending time with his family.

SPRING TRAINING SITES

1901	Norfolk, Virginia
1902–1904	Thomasville, Georgia
1905	Charleston, South Carolina
1906	Jacksonville, Florida
1907	Thomasville, Georgia
1908–1912	Augusta, Georgia
1913	Athens, Georgia
1914–1915	Macon, Georgia
1916–1918	Miami, Florida
1919–1920	Columbus, Georgia
1921	Galveston, Texas
1922–1937	St. Petersburg, Florida
1938–1940	Bradenton, Florida
1941	San Antonio, Texas
1942	Sanford, Florida
1943–1944	Wallingford, Connecticut
1946–1947	Fort Lauderdale, Florida
1948–1953	Bradenton, Florida

SOURCES

Buege, Bob. *The Milwaukee Braves: A Baseball Eulogy*. Milwaukee: Douglas American Sports Publications, 1988.

Caruso, Gary. *The Braves Encyclopedia*. Philadelphia: Temple Press, 1995.

Creamer, Robert W. *Stengel: His Life and Times*. New York: Simon and Schuster, 1984.

Kaese, Harold. *The Boston Braves, 1871–1953*. New Hampshire: Northeastern University Press, 1948.

Lowry, Philip J. *Green Cathedrals: The Ultimate Celebration of All Major League Ballparks*. New York: Walker Publishing Company, 2006.

ABOUT THE AUTHOR

William J. Craig resides in Revere, Massachusetts, with his wife, Charlene, and daughter, Meadow. He has written books *Fort Devens*, *Revere* and *Last Rites*. After serving in the U.S. Army and U.S. Air Force, he studied at Gordon College in Wenham, Massachusetts, and received a BA in history. He has been a loyal Braves fan since his youth.